MANAGEMENT
MUMBO-JUMBO

A Skeptics' Dictionary

Adrian Furnham

palgrave
macmillan

First published 2006 by
PALGRAVE MACMILLAN
Houndmills, Basingstoke, Hampshire RG21 6XS and
175 Fifth Avenue, New York, N.Y. 10010
Companies and representatives throughout the world

PALGRAVE MACMILLAN is the global academic imprint of the Palgrave
Macmillan division of St. Martin's Press, LLC and of Palgrave Macmillan Ltd.
Macmillan® is a registered trademark in the United States, United Kingdom
and other countries. Palgrave is a registered trademark in the European
Union and other countries.

ISBN-13: 978-1-4039-8702-0
ISBN-10: 1-4039-8702-5

This book is printed on paper suitable for recycling and
made from fully managed and sustained forest sources.

A catalogue record for this book is available from the British Library.

A catalogue record for this book is available from the Library of Congress

10   9   8   7   6   5   4   3   2   1
15   14   13   12   11   10   09   08   07   06

Printed in China

For A and B
and the hols, you see

Also by Adrian Furnham

MANAGEMENT AND MYTHS: Challenging Business Fads, Fallacies and Fashions

THE PEOPLE BUSINESS: Psychological Reflections on Management

LEARNING AT WORK: Excellent Practice for Best Theory (*with John Taylor*)

THE DARK SIDE OF BEHAVIOUR AT WORK: Understanding and Avoiding Employees Leaving, Thieving and Deceiving (*with John Taylor*)

Contents

Preface   xi

INTRODUCTION   1

    Fads in management   3
    Management science?   9
    Management training   10
    Assumptions about people   14
    Conclusion   15

Ability and ambition   17
Above the line   19
All interventions are equally effective   21
Atmospherics   23
Awards, citations and gongs   26

The blame culture   28
Breaking bad news   31
The bright boss   33

Casuistry, sophistry and spin   35
Choosing management courses   37
Compulsory training   40
Correcting cock-ups   42
The curse of perfectionism   44

Damned if you do and . . . don't   46
Dom and sub   48

Energy at work   50
Engagement to divorce   52
Evangelists at work   54
Everyone is a winner   56

Family business 58

From private to public 60

Fundamentalist gurus 62

The gullible executive 64

How not to use consultants 66

Human remains 68

Incommunicado 71

The incubation period 73

Inoculating the workforce 75

Integrity tests 77

Job fit in plain speak 80

Living in Sweden 83

Managing the post-materialist employee 85

Management psychiatry 88

Money as a motivator 92

Nepotism, corruption and incompetence 95

Networming 98

Nyet: stopping progress 100

Odd places: university management 102

Orality at work 105

Organizational defense mechanisms 107

Passive–aggressive bureaucrats 110

The personality of organizations 113

Professional recruiters 115

Protecting your legacy 117

A psychological MOT 119

Rank sensitivity 121

Recruitment to betrayal 123

A rock and a hard place 125

Seeking the savior 127

Shift work 129

Space exploration 131

Specialists and generalists 134

Speeches, sermons and seminar presentations 137

Striking a balance 139

The task and the process 141

Telephone tell-tales 143

Titular realities 145

Trust at work 147

Uncertainty avoidance 149

Understanding understatement 151

Why would anyone want to work for you? 153

Workplace spirituality 155

CONCLUSION **157**

Manifestos 157

Mantras 159

Missions 164

Preface

This book contains about 60 short essays or thought-pieces on management. They differ in length, topic and degree of frivolity, but not style, philosophy or purpose.

They are reflections of an academic who reads management books and both gives and receives management lectures, seminars and symposia. I am also occasionally asked my opinion on classical management problems like appraisal and selection, coaching and counseling, teaching and training. I am often surprised by the wisdom of the inexperienced and uneducated and vice versa.

I considered various options for the title of this book:

- People are our most costly asset
- People are our fastest depreciating asset
- People are coy, capricious and irascible
- Management fads, fashions and foibles
- Common-sense management
- Managers are from Pluto, workers from Uranus

Many of the entries in this book have appeared in one guise or another in newspapers, magazines or books. The *Daily Telegraph*, the *Financial Times* and *The Times* (of London) have for over a decade been happy to print my sideways observations on the world of business. Similarly magazines like *Across the Board, Human Resources, New Scientist, Spotlight* have regularly featured my pieces on management issues. Also I have published various books on the theme of mismanagement: *Business Watching*; *The Myths of Management*; *The Psychology of Managerial Incompetence*; *The Hapless, Hopeless and Helpless Manager*; *The 3D Manager*; *Dangerous, Derailed and Deranged*; *The Sad, Bad Manager*, and *The Incompetent Manager*. Most of the entries here have been edited, updated and (where appropriate) changed as I have changed my mind, which is difficult and quite unnatural in middle age.

The inspiration for the essays comes from many sources that reflect my role as lecturer, book reviewer, trainer and consultant. I regularly share platforms with all sorts of individuals – fellow professionals, motivational speakers, successful managers. I also have friends – many ex-academics – who are consultants, some of whom ask for my help. I spend most of the day reading. And in the course of these activities I hear, read and see things which attract my attention.

I like to think of myself as a disinterested skeptic, someone who is lucky enough to be outside looking in and trying to evaluate. I don't have to sell my time or skills. I have no silver or magic bullets to solve all intractable "Gordian" knot management problems, though I know many people who do. It is a luxury to be in this position but many argue it means I have insufficient "real world" experience to comment with authority.

I have seen fashions come and go and will, no doubt, see many more. This book is my reflections, reactions and ruminations of these issues. The essays are bite-size being mostly 1000 words or less. They are meant to challenge, entertain and even enlighten. I hope they succeed.

ADRIAN FURNHAM
Islington, London

Introduction

It has been said, probably correctly, that *man* is the principle syllable in *man*agement, where (of course) man stands for mankind or people. *Man*aging people can be difficult, demanding and demeaning. It can also be exciting, exhilarating and (always) exhausting. For every management problem there is a solution which is simple, quick, cheap . . . and wrong. Everybody wants easy, effective and efficient solutions to intractable problems. Trouble is, they don't exist. But there are, of course, useful books, courses and seminars which help to understand and solve management problems. There is, however, often a negative correlation between what they promise and what they deliver.

Many organizations take the business of training managers very seriously indeed. The military is a good example. Big international corporations, like oil or drug companies can have big, lavish "training centers" in which they hope to teach young managers and update older ones. Some organizations even produce their own "handbook" which pre- and proscribe what they believe to be good management techniques.

Management books and training courses look at such things as the "essential functions" of management like planning, costing and pricing, and so on. They also look at the manager's role and their supposed ideal competencies. Courses also try to encourage a fair degree of self-analysis helping the manager to appraise their preferences, abilities and values. Some consider how a manager might go about planning their career. Nearly all do some propaganda exercise about the organization itself. Management education is, ideally, both practical and relevant. Hence many of the criticisms of MBA courses. It should also be suitable to the group being trained. That's the theory at any rate.

But there are those from the *apprenticeship school of thought* who believe guided experience is far superior to formal (relatively short) training. There are many models of this. Traditionally journalists started out as "cub" reporters on obscure provincial papers. They began at the bottom often guided by a demanding but helpful "hard bitten hack" who gave excellent, firm-but-fair, feedback and guidance. And as skills (in interviewing, writing) were honed so they were given bigger assignments.

This means on-the-job, not in-the-classroom, training may be best. These two are, of course, not mutually exclusive. Classroom (or better, expensive country hotel) training has many advantages. It offers an opportunity to acquire abstract knowledge of theories. And as Kurt Lewin said there is nothing as practical as a good theory because it can explain important processes. Further, concepts, procedures and processes can be derived from theories. All management is helped by an understanding of the theory. Hence both the importance and popularity of those courses called things like "Financial management for non-finance people".

But classroom teaching allows reflection, rumination, time-out, to bring some meaning to the whole enterprise of what one is doing, when and why. It often offers an opportunity to look back *and* look forward. To retreat from the tyranny-of-the-urgent to contemplate the really important.

Equally it offers managers an opportunity to benchmark, "shoot the breeze" and compare themselves to their peers. Courses teach one about what others know and think which may be radically different from oneself. It is important to get some ideas of one's abilities and style and this is done most effectively by semi-formal educational opportunities.

Yet the central question remains: what should be on the syllabus? That is, what should we be teaching managers on these courses? What knowledge or skills should they be learning and when? Indeed we have to ask the question "Why do we need managers at all"? Dunham and Pierce (1989, pp. 21–2) believe there are six good reasons:

1. Managers ensure that an organisation serves its basic purpose – the efficient production of specific goods or services.
2. Managers design and maintain the stability of an organisation's operations.
3. Managers choose the strategies needed to keep an organisation adapting in a controlled way to its changing environment.
4. Managers ensure that an organisation serves the ends of the people who control it.
5. Managers are the key informational link between an organisation and its environment.
6. As formal authorities, managers are responsible for the operation of an organisation's status system and serve as symbols of the organisation in ceremonial activities.

That is a reasonable list and certainly a good reason why we should put effort into the selection and training of good managers. All organizations, even the most democratic, not-for-profit, organization, need leaders to manage their day-to-day affairs.

Fads in management

Fads over the last decade have been numerous. Managers are prone to fads, no doubt because management consultancy, trainers and writers are. They provide instant answers to complex questions. Shapiro (1996) pointed out fads in strategy (the need for vision and mission); in structure (flat, upside-down organizations); in motivation (empowerment); in customer focus and in techniques like Total Quality Management and Process Re-engineering. In a wonderfully witty way she defines (honestly and accurately) what many business terms really mean:

Accountability: A characteristic of which everyone else in the organisation needs far more. Not to be confused with Authority, which is what I need more of.

Benchmarking: 1. Comparison of operations against best-in-class; a superb way to spark new ideas and significant insights when the examples are selected with thought and imagination; 2. The basis for great jobs in which the incumbents have no substantive responsibilities other than to gallivant around the world, meet all sorts of interesting people, make occasional proclamations about all the neat things other companies do, and submit appropriately lavish expense reports.

Customer: 1. An inconvenience to the smooth functioning of a business; 2. A walking revenue stream, always susceptible to a better deal offered by another vendor.

Hierarchy: An inevitable component of organisations that can be misunderstood and mismanaged but cannot be abolished or obliterated, even if the pyramid is flattened, delayered, or turned on its side, or the language is tortured to prevent references to supervisors and subordinates.

Mission statement: 1. A short, specific statement of purpose, intended to serve as a loose musical score that motivates everyone to play the same tune without strict supervision; 2. Frequently, an assertion of undying commitment to some amalgam of "total quality," "low-cost producer," "empowered workforce," "excellence," "continuous improvement", and other bizbuz shibboleths that, although written for a specific organisation is equally applicable to an aircraft manufacturer, a software development firm, a community hospital, a department store chain, or the local dry cleaner; 3. In some companies, a talisman, hung in public spaces, to ward off evil spirits.

Opportunity: 1. A favourable circumstance, conducive to progress or advancement; 2. A euphemism, frequently used by consultants, to describe a problem or a threat.

Strategic plan: 1. A set of analyses, packaged in accordance with corporate requirements, that is undertaken in order to justify a campaign already under way or a budget about to be submitted; 2. (alt.) A set of analyses, packaged in accordance with corporate requirements, that nonetheless bears little or no resemblance to the real strategy being followed (but that, once printed and bound can, at a pinch, be used as a doorstop or a bookend).

All managers, indeed all employees, will no doubt enjoy the wickedly honest insights above. It is not difficult to be deeply cynical about business gurus and consultants.

But of course it is easy, and possibly unhealthy, to be too cynical. Cynicism eats one up. It poisons optimism, hope and motivation. But skepticism is often very healthy. Skepticism is critical doubt. It suggests that ideas are evaluated before they are adopted. It is anti-faddish. Hilmer and Donaldson (1996) notes five popular modern business concepts and why they can be misleading (pp. 3–5). They describe and the debunk some of the sacred cows of our time:

1. *Flatten the Structure.* Hierarchy is passé, flat is beautiful. Modern companies are like orchestras – one conductor and hundreds of players – not armies with long chains of command. Most organisations are hampered by too many levels of management between the board and the frontline employees who actually invent, make, sell, and provide services. Delayering – downsizing the ranks of middle management in particular – will improve communication, lower costs, speed up decision

making and better motivate all staff to contribute. Less management is better management. And fewer managers are the key.

2. *The Action Approach.* Don't become immobilised by planning and analysis – management is action, not study or reflection: "ready, fire, aim," "do it, fix it, try it," "inspire, empower, lead" rather than "deliberate and administer". Action is always better than the dreaded "paralysis by analysis". Successful managers get their people to move, and movement evolves into strategy as decisions are made in real time. People at the front line have good instincts, opinions of customers are the source of most marketing opportunities, and by stimulating action via empowerment, managers unleash the energy and ideas that are otherwise ignored and stultified by rigorous planning. Put another way, those managers left in the flat organisations of the future shouldn't try to plan, control, or think things through to any great level of detail. Instead, they should set visions, like the oracle of old, and urge the people into action, letting the decisions take shape over time. Intuition, not analysis, is the guiding light. Managers should be like Zen archers, letting the target draw the arrow to it.

3. *Techniques for All.* As problems arise, find the appropriate solution technique and apply it quickly. When the few managers left in place find that vision and intuition are not enough, the good manager need not go back to first principles or hard thinking but instead should pick up and religiously implement the "right" technique or program. This is "instant coffee" management – just open the can and add water – no work or thinking required. Modern approaches such as portfolio planning, value-based planning, niche strategies, total quality management, benchmarking, core process reengineering, and gain-sharing provide fast and reliable answers to all the tough questions, such as:
   a. What business are we really in and how do we compete?
   b. How can we get our staff to do things right the first time?
   c. How can we dramatically cut costs and waste?
   d. How can we provide the sales and service support our customers are demanding?
   e. How can we motivate people to innovate and contribute above and beyond the minimum demands of the job?

4. *The Corporate Clan*. Model the organisation to be more like a happy family than a hierarchy. Create a corporate culture that guides and encourages. Burn the rule books and procedures manuals. Operate as a clan, in which people understand through shared values what is right and wrong and what is good and bad. Rely on the culture to bring out the best in everyone. East is good, West is bad. They do it this way in Japan, and look at their successes – or the story goes.

5. *The Board of Directors as Watchdog*. Fix the board to better scrutinise management actions and decisions. Good management flows into the firm from the board of directors. Unless managers are under the continual scrutiny of a tough minded board of independent directors, they will fail to perform and, in the worst cases, steal the silver. It is argued that in many countries management has "captured" the board, which then becomes an acquiescent partner in schemes that enrich management or promote its interests ahead of those of shareholders. The remedy: separate the roles of chairman of the board and chief executives and then have the nonexecutive chairman supported by a board with a clear majority of outside part-time directors independent of management influence. The chief executive, and possibly one other executive such as the top financial officer or top operating executive, are the only managers who should be board members, and they ought not serve on committees dealing with board composition, executive remuneration, or auditing. In other words, good management depends on removing management's influence from the boardroom and leaving the direction of the corporation firmly in the hands of part-time outsiders.

The influence of the five false trails on management thought and practice is reflected in language. Contemporary management-speak has picked up ingredients of each of the trails. Many of these language shifts are positive, a response to changes in the forces that shape businesses, such as increased global competition and new information, communication, and production technologies. But in other respects, the changing language represents a pendulum that has swung too far toward simplifying and trivialising management, replacing ideas and actions based on sound reasoning with fads and dogma.

Rather than fad-adoption or management-bashing, Hilmer and Donaldson (1996) suggest one can take faddish ideas and concepts and see the positive idea underlying them. The authors give an excellent example on p. 9:

	False Trail	Positive Idea
Structure	Avoid formal structures, hierarchies, and accountabilities: be flexible, ad hoc	Actively use structure, hierarchy, and accountability to direct activities and shape behaviour
	Eliminate levels of management relentlessly: flatter is better	Beware of levels of management that add no value
Action	"Just do it"	Keep moving, but be aware of the basis of your actions
	Follow intuition and gut feelings: end "paralysis by analysis"	Respect analysis, data and reflection as well as intuition
	Keep experimenting, trying new ideas	Distinguish experiments from commitments
Techniques	Techniques provide effective answers	Stay abreast of techniques but be highly sceptical
	One technique suits most situations	Customize the techniques you select
	Keep up with the flow of new techniques	Limit the number of initiatives under way at any one time
Culture	Developing and sustaining culture is management's most critical task	Use clan ideas and culture selectively to reinforce priorities and encourage action
	Ensure that everyone in the organisation adopts the same culture	Encourage diversity by including various subcultures in the organisation
Board of Directors	Make sure the board keeps management honest and in check	Focus the board on enhancing corporate and top management performance
	Independence of directors are key	Competence and integrity of directors are key

And Hilmer and Donaldson (1996) present five helpful questions for every manager to ask him/herself (pp. 202–3):

1. Have you become preoccupied with downsizing, flattening, and informal work groups instead of aligning your structure and hierarchy with your goals?
    - When did you last use structure, hierarchy, and accountability to trigger and reinforce a major change or improvement?
    - Can you describe how each level in your organisation adds value to the level below, and do the managers at each level understand their different tasks and accountabilities? Have you given your formal structure a fair chance to work for you?

2. Have you been cutting back on data, staff and analysis to the point where you are beginning to feel uncomfortable about decisions you are making? Are you concerned that there are not sufficient solid reasons behind your actions? Are you sure your organisation deeply understands its customers, markets, technologies and economics?

   ■ Do people in your organisation look down on those who say, "Time out" or "We really ought to get more data?"

   ■ Can you distinguish experiments from commitments?

   ■ What was the last key experiment you conducted, and what did you learn?

3. Has your organisation become increasingly attracted to techniques?

   ■ Are there a large number of techniques being used around your company and are these techniques often dropped after a year or so?

   ■ Are increasing numbers of managers going to short seminars offering quick fixes as opposed to more substantive and less prescriptive courses on management?

   ■ When your organisation applies a technique, is a significant effort made to customize the technique so that the forms, questions, data requests, meetings, and decision processes fit into the way your organisation works and make sense to your people?

4. Are "We need to strengthen or change our culture" and "It's all culture" becoming your main remedies to problems with service, quality, motivation or communication?

   ■ Can you describe instances of how performance at the front line has been significantly changed because of some initiative with respect to culture?

   ■ How well does your organisation deal with the diversity and potential diversity of its work force? Is the prevailing culture a help or hindrance in this regard?

5. Is the board mainly a watchdog and controller? Is it spending most of its time on conformance issues? Has it set believable overall performance goals for the company, and does it take achievement of these goals seriously?

   ■ Is the board's agenda dominated by conformance issues such as audit, legal matters, formal approval of decisions and reports, and compliance reviews?

- Are directorships in your firm seen as sinecures, or is each director widely recognised as bringing first-rate competence and integrity to the deliberations of the board?
- When did your board of directors last assess its own contribution to the performance of the organisation?

A sensible, sobering and important list of questions every manager should be required to answer.

Management science?

There are dozens of big, heavy, textbooks on management for students of the discipline. They start off by defining what management is. They are told it is the rather nebulous but all-encompassing activity/process of planning, directing and controlling organizational resource in the pursuit of goals. It's the process of optimizing financial, human and material facets of the organization to achieve its goal.

Management is part art, part science, part profession. Managers, we are told, need very specific skills: administrative, analytical, communicative, conceptual, decision-making, human relations, technical. They spend their time controlling work activities, solving problems; planning work activities; communicating up (to seniors) across (to colleagues), down (to staff), both formally and informally; coaching others, and so on.

Essentially management is about keeping the organization going . . . indefinitely. They must therefore anticipate depression, recession, fashion changes, political changes and political attack. Managers have to be cunning. They often have to get superior performance from average people.

But which part is management and science and which part art? Does it really matter? The question usually opens up an undergraduate-level argument about what is science, then degenerate into "Does it matter?" Can we have management science?

Nachmias and Nachmias (1981) list six criteria or axioms:

- Behavior is orderly and regular: there is a pattern to behavior that can be understood (predicted and measured).
- We can understand behavior/know nature: we can, through observation and experimentation, come to understand the causes of behavior.

- Relative knowledge to superior ignorance: scientific knowledge is incomplete, tentative and changing, not absolute.
- Natural phenomena have natural causes: no supernatural explanation for behavior need be posited.
- Nothing is self-evident: all claims for scientific truth need to be demonstrated objectively.
- Scientific knowledge is acquired from empirical observation and experiments.

Scientific empiricism involves making observations that meet the following criteria:

- They are objective. That is, they are not influenced by any preconceived ideas about how the results "should" turn out. Patterns may be observed by anybody.
- They are systematic. Observations or experiments should be carried out in an orderly way; for example, when observing behavior, experimenters should know exactly what behaviors they are looking for and how to record them accurately. Disciplined observation is crucial.
- They are replicable. All observations can be repeated by others, with the same results. Even if an observation is done objectively and systematically, the results are suspect if they cannot be obtained by others. If results are not replicable they are not reliable and not universally true.

To all intents and purposes management science is a perfectly respectable social science. The top papers in the area are as good as found anywhere. But business managers and (alas) often business-school academics are more interested in application than basic science. The two are, inevitably, closely related. But observation and experimental work are necessary. The famous Hawthorne study from which we get the Hawthorne Effect was an experiment. There is serendipity in science.

Management training

It's easy to be dismissive about management ideas and training. It has been suggested that management is really about the art of looking for trouble, supposedly finding it whether it exists or not, diagnosing its cause incorrectly and then applying the wrong remedy to cure it!

For many, management is the device put into place that makes it difficult for people to work. Or else a manager is little more than an administrative assistant with a big office/space.

Politicians always win approval for claiming to find the money to spend on public services by "culling bureaucrats". They perceive the anti-management zeitgeist whose mantra is managers breed – there are too many of them and they need culling. Management is really quite simple and therefore can be done by fewer, less well trained and less well paid people. Managers are untrustworthy and motivated only by self-interest.

Management baiting is a good sport. There appears to be a continuing, low-key and low-quality, vociferous and vituperous "debate" on the usefulness of middle-aged, middlebrow, middle managers in big public organizations. Trimming bloated overheads and headquarters staff are good vote winners.

Three things strike the outsider when looking in on management education:

1. It's all common sense, isn't it?

   That is, experience, intuition and modern technology is essentially all you need to get on in business. Management education is an expensive, pointless exercise that needs to be abandoned. Managers must be taught technology because that is important but all the rest is really just common sense. But this begs the question as to the origin of common sense itself. Where does it come from? Why do some people have more of it than others? Can it be tested for?

2. Reheating and relabeling.

   Management is certainly prone to fad and fashion. Every so often simple, possibly profound, ideas have to repackaged in the language and style of the day. So charm became social skills became emotional intelligence becomes . . .

3. Proof, science and evidence.

   It is all very well being handed down "the wisdom of the ages" but a sneaking suspicion that confronts many people is that the tactics don't work: the ideas are false; the science is true. What we desperately need, but clearly do not have, is evidence-based management. There is, for many management ideas, absence of evidence rather than evidence of absence.

But some ideas in management are simply wrong. They are based on false assumptions. What is wrong with management science or organizational behavior as it is taught in business schools?

Furnham (2004) also offered various specific accusations that can be made against the business school discipline of organizational behavior as currently taught (pp. 432–3).

1. *Political correctness:* This involves anything from a doctrinaire denial of biological influences on human behaviour to laments about the fashion-ably oppressed workers or consumers. Organisational behaviour writers and teachers seems particularly eager to jump on any politically correct bandwagon, like diversity, espousing the accepted view of following lay enthusiasms like emotional intelligence. Fashion and managerial acceptance, not veridicality, seem the important criteria for researching and writing about a topic, which is not how science should or does pro-ceed. Often fairly "thin" ideas like management-by-walking-about are picked up and dropped by fickly consultants and researchers more eager to please managers and fit in with the zeitgeist than "do science".

2. *Anecdotes not data:* There is too much emphasis on stories, case stud-ies, parables and anecdotes and not enough emphasis on the data to substantiate theories and concepts. Case studies make interesting read-ing and they are extremely useful for teaching. But science develops from hunch to hypothesis to theory to law. We move from observation and induction to verification and falsification. Organisational behav-iour researchers need to develop and test theories more. They need to understand the power of statistical modelling rather than mere case study accumulation. A good example can be seen in Goleman's (1995) phenomenally successful book on Emotional Intelligence. Whilst the author has a PhD in Psychology he is a science journalist and has the craft of the story teller. Various often quite unrelated studies are quoted, the book tells stories about the topic. The academics have been late in catching up trying to "unpack" the concept and understand where it fits in the established "periodic table" of individual differ-ences. However, lack of theoretical clarity as well as good measures prevented neither lecturers nor consultants enthusiastically propagat-ing the very simplistic and often muddled ideas of the book.

3. *No powerful theories:* A theory is a network of falsifiable causal general-isations. But organisational behaviour has a messy stew of ideology, buzz words and doctrinaire statements. What theory regularly leads to

is the prediction of empirical relationships and generalisations across topics/phenomena. Theories in psychology and economics – dissonance theory, equity theory, social exchange theory – are warmly embraced but never bettered by organisational behaviour theories.

4. *Derivative methodology:* Most psychologists collect their own data to test hypotheses. They choose the most appropriate methods to do so. Many economists analyse others' large data sets with sophisticated econometric models. Organisational behaviour researchers often do neither. The focus should be on what we know rather than how we found out about it. Methodology is a tool, but an important one for doing research. Organisational behaviour research is difficult – there are lots of related and confounding factors, but organisational behaviour really needs to explore them sensitively and thoroughly through advanced empirical methodologies.

5. *Identity:* Organisational behaviour does not know what it is and what it isn't. Its incoherence means it never rejects ideas, many of which are pretentious and shallow. Marxists, feminists, psycho-biologists, ethno-methodologies, all can find a cosy nest in a course or book on organisational behaviour. Everybody is welcome, all ideas are equally important and all approaches are equally good. There are no rules, no limits and no quality control as long as one is politically correct (see above). All this exacerbates the identity problem of what the topic and mission of their enterprise is at its core.

6. *Marketing:* OB teachers, however, certainly know about marketing their ideas. They know the power of the press, the virtue of spin and they use it to the full to further their cause. Organisational behaviour courses are well attended and organisational behaviour departments are often highly rated within business schools (at least by the students) because of the business that they attract. Marketing is important because often the ideas are ephemeral and vaporous – there is a constant need for marketing because there are constantly new products on the market.

7. *Attempting tractable rather than important problems:* Researchers know the difference between tractable, and those intractable, but perennial, problems of business that are pretty unsolvable. So they go for those pretty important ones where they can make a difference. And this is a fairly good strategy. To make a small but significant difference is surely the right thing to do.

Assumptions about people

Is there a new managerial philosophy which believes (seriously) in growing and investing in people (at work) development. Miles and Snow (1994)
believe there are ideological, societal and technological forces that are
leading to a new human investment philosophy which they describe in
8 points (p.146):

1. Most people not only want to contribute and have untapped
    capabilities.
2. Most people are trustworthy as well as trusting in their relationships.
3. The manager's basic task is to prepare the organisation's human and
    technical resources to respond effectively and efficiently.
4. The manager must make both current and long-term investments in
    technical skills for every organisational member.
5. The manager must invest in employees' long term growth and developing
    competence.
6. Managers must be prepared to make investments in both technical and
    governance skills across organisational units within other network
    member firms.
7. Investments in human capabilities, including self-governance compe-
    tence, builds adaptive capacity and creates a learning organisation.
8. The more competent the manager's own organisation, the more facile
    and effective are the network linkages it can make.

It is a long time since the old days of theory X and theory Y: the idea
that people have underlying assumptions about workers either being
essentially good vs essentially bad.

But the issue lives on. Take for instance the problem with company theft.
People steal at work – they steal cash, goods, time, and so on. Some jobs,
often badly paid, tedious jobs, offer many opportunities to "liberate" goods
in order to supplement a meager income. Supermarkets lose millions as do
some factories. The question is how to prevent or at least limit the problem.

Pessimists turn to technology, optimists to discussion. Pessimists
believe most workers are "chancers and opportunists"; probably basically
dishonest and happy to rip off customers and their company for as much as
they can get. Hence managers install cameras, x-ray machines and tags to

monitor staff and goods. This is seen to be the best way to deal with the problem.

Optimists believe thieving is done by a small minority or by bad management or by sloppy procedures. They know that "shrinkage" is bad for everyone. So they call meetings, describe the problem and encourage everyone to "have their say" in dealing with it. Most of us, they argue, are poorer as a result of this. So let us discuss the cause and the cure together.

The optimistic–pessimistic dimension is probably too simple, though it does capture a lot in the assumptions managers make about their staff, and those made by the staff about their managers. Other factors include whether people are easily changeable, trainable or not; whether there really are sex, age, race differences that affect behavior at work, and so on.

Some believe that work can never be made satisfying; others that work is a major source of psychological benefit. Some are materialists, others post-materialists in their view of the function of society, the role of having vs being, and the extent to which money, power and possessions bring happiness.

Inevitably senior managers in organizations share similar assumptions, expectations and values. It is part of the selection and socialization process. And it has powerful effects on how one manages. It's no bad idea to confront these assumptions once in a while.

Conclusion

One of the problems of the world of management is low *cost to entry* for advisers. Practically anybody can call themselves and try to pass off as a management consultant, a business guru or a people expert. After all most adults have had some experience of both being managed and managing. And curiously the market seems ever buoyant for the services of "expert" advisers. In good times they can propound every wacky idea to make one even richer, while in bad times they happily portray themselves as having the secret knowledge for survival. Willing buyers and willing sellers make for a good market.

Some management ideas, techniques and processes are extremely useful and fundamentally important. They always have been and they always will be. It is true that the world of work is changing: how and where we work as well as fundamentally what we do. Technology, market forces, shifting centers of finance and manufacturing all make a difference. And personal values and expectations have changed. But still there remain fundamental truths about managing people in all jobs in all societies over time. People want to know what is expected of them and they constantly need different types of support. They value being valued and are sensitive to favoritism, bias and dishonesty.

There may be many ideas that sound old-fashioned, like, managing by objectives, but they contain fundamental truths. Equally, thriving on chaos, finding your inner child and encouraging spiritual awareness are perhaps less important concepts or ideas.

Classic management ideas and concepts may not sound sexy and sell books but many have stood the test of time. They need refreshing, repackaging and rediscovering surely. But beware the magic bullet of the peddler of high promise mumbo-jumbo. It may mean nothing more than that rapid, large and dramatic transfer of funds from your company into theirs.

References

Dunham, R. and Pierce, J. (1989). *Management.* London: Scott, Foresman & Co.

Furnham, A. (2004). The future (and past) of work psychology and organisational behaviour. *Management Review, 15,* 420–36.

Hilmer, F. and Donaldson, D. (1996). *Management Redeemed: Debunking the fads that undermine corporate performance.* New York: Free Press.

Nachmias, G. and Nachmias, D. (1981). *Research Methods in the Social Sciences.* London: Edward Arnold.

Miles, R. and Snow, C. (1994). *Fit, Failure and the Hall of Fame.* New York: Free Press.

Shapiro, E. (1996). *Fad Surfing in the Boardroom.* London: Capstone.

Ability and ambition

Fancy being a guru or a management consultant? Easy. First start by drawing a square. Then subdivide it by mid-point vertical and horizontal lines drawing a box with four squares. This is a famous 2 × 2. Now we need H for high and L for low above top left and top right; as well as top and bottom vertical lines.

OK? Now for the theory (in fact any theory). Above the top H and L write *ability* and between the H and L on the side write *ambition*. So now we have four types. And there is "the model". Now all you have to do is describe the four types, how they behave and how to manage them.

Of the four squares two are always pretty straightforward. They are always the consistent high/high or low/low boxes. So in this example they refer to people who are both *or* neither able or ambitious. Thus high/high people are good news. They have capacity, skill and knowledge. And presumably their ambitions drive them to be hard-working, achievement-oriented and the like. They are potentially high-flyers.

The war for talent is about finding and holding on to these motivated and capable people. One should however look carefully into the nature and ultimate goal of their ambition . . . which may make then less attractive.

The low/low people are bad news. Talentless and feckless. Little ability and little ambition to exploit what little ability they have. They are very clearly from the select out-group. They can be perfectly able, steady and reliable blue-collar workers but not helpful support staff for entrepreneurial offices where people are expected to "muck in" and stay late in busy times.

But this is where it becomes interesting. What explains the seeming paradox of people in the other two boxes. First high/low – the personnel with great ability and little ambition. There may be many explanations. They may not be fully aware of their abilities, having never had an opportunity to evaluate or test them. Or their environment may not allow for their development and exploitation. It may be that they are lazy or content or likely to inherit much money or property.

They could however be fruitfully reminded of the parable of the talents (Matthew 25:14) where people are instructed not to ignore, downplay or waste their unique (God-given) talents. But people need to know both how to find out what they are good at, and what to do to realize their talents.

Secondly, there is the sadder and often problematic individual with great ambition but little talent. They have probably graduated with distinction from self-esteem courses but flunked school and other "educational opportunities". Much of course depends on what they are ambitious for. And it depends on what you could describe as talent or ability.

In nearly all jobs there is a positive correlation between cognitive ability and success (however that is measured). One exception is sales: you need confidence, a modicum of charm and resistance (ego strength) as much as anything else. Salespeople need robust self-belief and the ability to triumph over frequent setback and rejection. All the more important as everyone is a salesperson today.

The crucial questions that remain are four-fold. Where do abilities come from (nature or nurture)? How do people discover their abilities? What are the origins of ambition? Can or does ambition dry up? A pity the model does not answer those questions.

But consultants and trainers know that people really love these simple categorical models. The really clever ones try three dimensions and the result is a cube. But somehow it's too difficult to think of eight types some of whom are high, low, high and others low, high, low.

So we return to the 2 × 2. One trainer collects these much as people collect beer mats or match boxes. It seems that most problems can be described in these categorical terms. Most people know about the SWOT Model (Strengths, Weaknesses, Opportunities, Threats).

The trouble of course is that typologies are so crude. Very, very few human characteristics fit neatly into two types. Even sex and perhaps right or left hand preference, which seem obvious examples, don't quite fit the bill. People differ on dimensions. Height, intelligence and so on are linear concepts. Whilst we may talk about tall and short people or bright and dull managers, we know these are based on either arbitrary or population based statistics.

So within each box there remains great variety. Thus in the high, high box there may be a very, very ambitious and quite able manager who is subtly and importantly different from a pretty ambitious and extremely able manager. Ah, so what one does is split each box into two.

Much depends on the observation that there are two types of people in the world. Those who believe there are two types and those that don't.

Above the line

The concept of above or below the line occurs in many contexts. In bridge scoring, for instance. There are of course many other important "line" references. The British army has the "thin red line". In rugby you line up at "line-outs". Organizations try to be aligned so that they all point in the same direction. If you "step out of line" you may be given lines. You "draw a line" in the sand.

In marketing there are a lot of line references. There is above the line which is mass marketing: scatter-gun, broad based marketing through the big media like radio and television. Below the line is targeted to a more specialist audience – a very specific message to a special group for a specific purpose. The latter takes more money, time and preparation.

But being marketers they have of course come up with very different line related concepts. Do they now talk about "through the line" – integrated marketing which does not distinguish between above and below the line? There is also a concept called "behind the line". This is guerrilla marketing – the paid graffiti artist, the people putting naughty ads in phone booths, stickers on benches.

In business you have a line manager though you may also have a dotted-line relationship. This all refers to the organizational chart: the organogram of power. Lines tend to be horizontal and vertical only.

Flat organizations which are the current fad have fewer horizontal lines. But these lines are terribly important. There are nearly always lines to separate three groups: the grown-ups – the Board, the Pantheon, the Cabinet, the top Johnnies, often no more than a dozen or so and the senior/general managers. Below them there are the junior managers, senior supervisors. And below them are the workers, the foot soldiers, the customer-facing staff and the like. There are also support staff, represented by four or five pretty crucial (horizontal) lines.

When HR people and management gurus talk of organizations and personal development, these lines really matter. In fact it is possible that the concept of development is simply dropped for people below some designated line. They do not need, or are perceived not to want personal development.

A great deal of money is spent on recruitment and development for people above the line. Head-hunters or "search consultants" as they prefer to be called now, take a reasonable percentage of quite a large number to help you fill your crucial position.

And for personal development your above-the-line manager may have a personal coach (at £300 an hour) or attend extremely expensive business-school based courses to do a bit of networking, reflection and self-awareness training.

Paradoxically perhaps the assessment budget is the other way around. Graduates are put through very expensive assessment centers. Junior managers may have to complete various exercises including work sample try-outs and be intensively grilled in interviews by many staff.

But it is very unlikely that very senior staff are assessed with anything more than a long interview. Recruiters rely on the CV and their informants (the 360-degree rating providers) for data. It's all reputational. Hence the importance of seriously guarding your reputation and being nice to people as you climb the greasy pole to success.

Crossing the line sure makes a difference. Different rules apply – the class of travel, the size of office, the type of support staff.

Ostentatious senior management privileges are, however, rather out of date. So you have to be more guarded, even secretive, lest the media find out. The posh dining rooms have gone, even the generously spaced offices. But you can spend a great deal on executive development, as it is seen to be really crucial to the business.

So no wonder people are eager to cross certain organizational lines. They know that it makes all the difference to be above the salt.

All interventions are equally effective

Doctors call them *placebo* effects while psychologists call them *non-specific* effects. In education they are called the *inspirational teacher* effect. But the news has not got through to the business world. And too many consultants want to keep it that way.

This is the story. When trying to determine the efficacy of a treatment or course it is important to distinguish between two different factors. The first are called direct *specific effects*. That means the type of treatment. For the medic it may be quite different drugs or methods of treating the same problem. For the psychologist it may be using a Freudian psychoanalytic versus a cognitive behavior therapy approach to a phobic or depressed patient. For the teacher it may be trying to teach the same topic in seminars versus lectures, or by case studies versus principles.

And for the business person it means using quite varied techniques like quality circles or 360-degree feedback to managers, or introducing self-directing, empowered teams to solve similar problems in productivity.

Specific effects are observed when different medicines, treatments, courses, interventions have quite different effects. People become zealous proselytizers of their method. They become believers in their theory, therapy and application, believing *only* it works best.

But there are also *non-specific effects* in medicine, therapy, education and business. Non-specific effects arise as a result of the intervention, whatever form that happened to take. They are sometimes called the therapist effect, though they could equally be called the consultant effect. They are also sometimes called the allegiance effect.

What this means is that the relationship with the therapist, teacher, consultant is a powerful force in the ultimate efficacy of the outcome. They help by giving the client positive expectations. They help by making them focus on their problems. They help by giving considerable support (social, emotional, informational). And they help by getting involved in shared goals and activities.

What studies of psychotherapy have revealed seems contradictory at first. It is that *all* therapies are equally effective (the specific effects are trivial). But the non-specific effects account for success. That is, it is not *what* is done, but *who* does it and *how*.

Consider the four factors shown to be powerful predictors of psychotherapy success. And ponder whether this is exactly what happens in consultant–client relationships. First, a positive but emotionally charged, confiding relationship with a helping persona. That is, the relationship is powerful, close and affective, leading to some sort of bond. Next, the setting is one of renewal, change, healing, novelty. Third, that the consultant provides a theory, an explanation (even a myth) that describes both how problems arose in the first place and how to cure or resolve them. This is, of course, the magic bullet – which is the non-effective specific effect. But it is the belief in the efficacy of the effect rather than the effect itself which is the powerful ingredient.

Lastly, the consultant needs to endorse, demand or even take part in a ritual, rite or procedure with the client that is (supposedly) believed by both to be efficacious. The more psychobabbly the gobbledegook the better. But the ritual, whatever it is, has to fit the zeitgeist.

The scientific literature on psychotherapy shows two things, both fairly indigestible to many in the business. First, that the training of people makes very little difference to their efficacy and patient outcomes. This in effect means you have it or you haven't and training does not instil it. Next that the therapist is more important than the therapy. The intervener is more important than the intervention. The consultant, more important than the change process.

What all this means is well known to insightful managers and good consultants. Success is a matter of relationships. The inspirational teacher is inspirational, irrespective of the topic or subject of that inspiration. Whatever one might believe or want to believe about the power of a particular strategy to effect change and benefits in an organization, it is the case that most work or don't work equally well.

There are no magic bullets but there are magic marksmen. Choose your consultant with care. It is your relationship with them and their skill, charisma and charm that really does the business.

Atmospherics

How do you design shops and arrange products to maximize sales? Supermarkets know the importance of layout. Shoppers are confronted first by fresh produce to convince them that they need a trolley rather than a basket. Then the staples – bread and milk – are often furthest away from the entrance and each other to make customers walk the aisles.

There is now a small army of experts who determine what is arranged, where and why. There are blue lights above the meat counter to make the meat look redder, but yellow lights in the fresh bread and cakes section to emphasize the golden nature of that product. Some products that go together are side by side (tea and coffee, butter and cheese) but dried fruit can be anywhere and Marmite hidden with jams and preserves rather than sharing shelf space with its savory soulmates.

Time spent in any shop is the best predictor of how much money is spent there. So shop designers are in the business of slowing you down and making you walk the length and breadth of the shop to find what you want. Mirrors slow people down, hence their popularity in department stores.

The idea is to increase impulse buying. But researchers have found that you need to get people in the right mood to maximize the effect. The window shopper, the harassed executive and the purposeful, list-driven, pragmatist can all be persuaded to dally, inspect and purchase when the right mood is created.

So how to quickly (cheaply and efficiently) change mood? The answer is in smells and music. Both have immediate associations. They have been described as emotional provocateurs. They seem to be both powerful and primitive. And they appear to work at an unconscious level.

Studies have shown that if you match music and product, people buy more. Play French accordion music in a wine shop and sales of French wine increase. Play stereotypic German bierkeller music and the Riesling flies off the shelves at twice the speed.

Music has powerful emotional associations and memories. Know an individual and you can induce happiness and sadness, pride and shame, sentimentality and coolness. The Scots fight better to the sound of the pipes, the English to the British Grenadiers.

Music is used to quicken the heart and the pace (marching music) as well as to relax. Few state occasions or indeed any with rites-de-passage significance take place without music to signify the mood and meaning of the occasion.

But the scientists are now beginning to play with smell or, if you prefer, aroma. It is now perfectly feasible to develop cheap, synthetic but impressively realistic scents of anything you fancy. Baking bread, warm chocolate, pine forests, sea breezes, new car smell, or mown grass – it is all possible!

These new smells can be pumped into buildings at various points to maintain a consistent pong. And we have come a long way from chemically lemon-scented lavatory cleaner or sandalwood joss sticks.

Smells can make you hungry, or relaxed, or even cross. Some researchers have attempted to use smells to increase sales. They found the best smell to pump into a petrol-station minimart was "starched sheet smell". Why? The answer appears to be that garage forecourts are dirty, oily places and that people have a clear concern with the cleanliness of the foodstuff (especially fresh pastries) in the shop. The exceptionally clean association of starched sheets does the business. People's concern disappears and they buy more.

The idea is simple. Smells have associations, some of which are shared. Buildings such as hospitals and rooms like dentists' surgeries have distinct smells that can almost induce phobia. Christmas has its own smell, as does the seaside.

But individuals too have specific smell associations. Thus unique smells like Earl Grey tea, Pear's soap, or particular perfumes can have unusual effects on individuals. And the same smell can have opposite effects on two people. The smell of tea can bring pain and pleasure: memories of boredom and excitement.

We know that smell is generationally linked as a result of shared product experience and lifestyle. Far fewer people bake bread or live in the country than used to. Hence the comforting feeling associated with the scents of warm bread, or cut hay, or fresh horse manure may work on people of only a particular age cohort.

Music and smell work on mood. And moods don't last long, though they can profoundly influence both thinking (decision-making) and behavior (shopping). The process can even be semi-subliminal: while people are initially aware of particular scents, they remain unaware of how their purchasing behavior is changed.

Scientists are beginning to become more interested in this curious backwater. Those studying attraction (the effects of body odor), decision-making and brain chemistry are curious as to precisely what physiological consequences occur once positive and negative moods are induced and familiar scents are detected. But they still do not know how people are able to distinguish between pepper and peppermint, or how wine tasters do their job. It was not thought of as a very serious area of enquiry until the commercial consequences were spelled out.

It is possible to imagine many positive and negative consequences of increasing our knowledge of the link between atmospherics and mood, and mood and behavior. Some will object to a 21st century version of a new "hidden persuader"; others will be pleased to find someone has thought to ionize and aromatize their working, traveling and shopping environment.

Awards, citations and gongs

Lots of organizations believe, quite rightly, in celebrating success. Recognition of good performance can take many forms: dinners, work outings, days off for whole groups who "did well" by hitting or exceeding targets and expectations.

Celebrating success is seen to be motivating. It is also for those who believe in equity theory seen to be just. Success is rewarded.

It is also possible to isolate and name specific individuals. Armies give medals, governments give gongs, schools give prizes. The best are held up as exemplars of excellence. Models for the masses.

So periodically lists are posted of individuals who are ordained the successful. Alas, human nature, being what it is, means that not everybody appears overjoyed at the prospect of seeing peers put forward. Jealousy, envy, pride and a host of other rather unattractive emotions frequently occur after the listing of the great and the good.

Lists of the successful can be seen as quite just and fair. Those who deserve to be there are there, and those who are not do not appear. But most people have questioned the possibility that errors, omissions and "corruption" may have occurred.

There are two problematic possibilities. The first is that there are those on this list who should not be there. Second, there are those not listed who should be.

Reading through the biannual honors list frequently surprises the middle-aged, middle-brow and middle manager who has probably bumped into a few nominees in their time. Be they academics, actors, business or sports people there is often the same surprise – why him or her?

The more unclear or fuzzy the criteria for nomination, the more the puzzle. And soon the specter of bribery, corruption, nepotism and the like appears. Whilst it is perfectly clear why Mr X is there, it is a complete mystery why Mr Y is on the list. What precisely did they do to receive this nomination? Who exactly was on the committee which made the decision?

Those on the list usually can indulge in that smug, self-satisfied certainty that their abilities, effort and hard work have been justly recognized. Some, however, may also query others' nominations. The more on the list, the less exclusive.

There is of course another group. Those not on the list who should be. Why is old Mr Z passed over year after year? What did they do to provoke the ire or ignorance of those making the decisions?

For many people this question refers to themselves though they are, no doubt, loathe to admit it. Talking to the "passed over and the pissed-off" often reveals that they have surprisingly little or distorted data on the criteria of success or indeed their place in the rank order. Many can be frighteningly ignorant about how they stack up in the realm of things.

There is another interesting anomaly in this prize game. Those who turn them down. In Britain awards are becoming a particularly hot political potato. But rejection has been going on for ages. All through the last century people turned down awards for various political and personal reasons. Others have accepted their awards and subsequently "given them back" when the awarding institutions did (or did not do) something they disapproved of. Soldiers returned their medals, academics their honorary degrees as a protest.

The business then of simply awarding prizes to the best, seen as both simple and motivational, can be fraught with problems. Whilst some see the whole process as beneficial and an inspiration for all, others see it as deeply divisive.

So certain schools and public bodies do either "prizes for all" or "prizes for none". They appear to endorse the old "tall poppy" syndrome of the Australians, meaning that the really successful are cut down to size. This is in effect punishing the successful.

The prizes for all schools argue that giving prizes might motivate the best, but it demotivates the majority, who are less successful. They come from the self-esteem school which argues, happily data-free, that success comes from positive self-esteem rather than the other way around. So they eschew awards for fear of what it might do to the unsuccessful.

Who would have thought that something so obviously straightforward could possibly become so complicated?

The blame culture

"Where there's blame, there's a claim". The blame culture has crossed the Atlantic. The old-fashioned Shackleton-epitomized virtues of endurance, fortitude and stoicism are but memories. "Screwing the system", that battle-cry of the sixties is now a baby boomer and generation-X pastime.

But who is to blame for the blame culture? Some of the culprits are easy to identify, but the more insidious much harder to spot. The first is of course *lawyers*. Litigation can be good business for an increasing army of lawyers though they have to sort through a large number of time-wasters before they get to those with a winnable case which brings them their bread and butter.

The second group must be *entrepreneurs* who start companies with one eye on the libel suit aimed to exploit this market. Like all entrepreneurs, they spot a "gap in the market" and new trend and off they go.

Thirdly, one may point the finger at *celebrities* who endorse these companies. They appear to make the idea of suing one's doctor, one's boss, one's "anything" respectable. They normalize the process: no longer bizarre, unheard of, inappropriate, abnormal.

And we now see the consequences. Innocent pastimes of one's childhood are now banned. Everyday in the newspapers there appear more and more stories of schools, councils and hospitals banning various activities lest they are sued. And now we are, at last, seeing the government trying to curtail the worst of the abusers.

But why has this occurred? Is it motivated by greed or anger? Is it purely a function of American-style litigation mania transferred to our shores? Is it a manifestation of the fall in trust we have with all our institutions? Is it a change in expectations?

Have we, as Prince Charles has suggested, raised expectations too high for young people who now believe ability and capacity for hard work are not necessary for success in life? Is everyone entitled to anything they want and will blame others (never themselves) if they don't get it? Or have we broken a vicious self-fulfilling prophesy process where young people without self-esteem or ambition never really exploit their talents?

Or is it a change in the zeitgeist? Psychologists call it attribution theory. It is the study of how people attribute blame, cause and responsibility. It is said that we can have healthy and unhealthy attributional styles. Unhealthy styles lead to depression, inertia and victimhood, but healthy attribution styles are related to motivation, resilience and happiness.

The idea is this: if you attribute success to luck, fate and chance (uncontrollable, external, global forces) but failure to personal factors like ability, motivation and the like, you will be prone to depression. Such people see the world as capricious and feel helpless, hapless and hopeless.

On the other hand, the pattern associated with mental health is to accept success as rightly due to personal effort, ability and talent and failure to luck, change or powerful others. So people are taught to externalize failure. In short, to blame others.

Why did you fail your maths O level? Healthy response: bad teaching, unfair paper, sickness at the time, change in syllabus, and so on. Unhealthy answer: I am not too bright, not good with maths, and so on.

It is, of course, more complicated than this but people do search for explanations and attributions. Newspaper reporters and television inter-viewers frequently ask quite badly "Who do you blame for this event?" Cause, responsibility and blame may be related, but as all lawyers know they are subtly different. And often, events have many causes including the well-known let-out, an "act of God".

Of course no sensible person or therapist would do it like that. They would examine and then challenge an unhealthy or self-defeating attribution style, trying to unpick its origins and consequences, and the extent to which it had some realistic basis. The idea is to be realistic not fantastic.

The self-esteem movement has tried to raise the performance, particu-larly of disadvantaged young people, by changing their attribution patterns. The theme is – make people feel confident, give them self-worth, raise their self-esteem and they will do well. Self-esteem, they argue, leads to success and not vice versa.

And paradoxically some of the original researchers in this area have tried to explain the rise in adolescent depression and suicide to their being over-praised and being taught ultimately maladaptive attribution patterns.

Indeed, it seems as if the social scientists and their fellow-travelers got the direction of causality wrong. Help people be successful and their attributions follow. Work on attributions alone and you may get young people whose expectations far exceed their ability and motivational capacity.

And you raise self-esteem in part by attributional therapy – that is, a train-ing in praise and blame. Viewers to talent shows (especially on television) are often perplexed by the reactions of relatively talentless performers who are given some clear, unequivocal feedback about their lack of ability. Presumably they have been carefully nurtured in the blame-culture therapy school to improve their self-esteem and refuse to believe their failure is their fault.

Humility has given way to hubris.

Breaking bad news

All managers have on occasions to break bad news. News about redundancy, mergers, acquisitions, corporate change and failure to be promoted. They may have to sack individuals, counsel others and deal with accidents. There may be groups of people involved, individuals, or more often both.

Breaking bad news is a skill. Nobody likes doing it. But to hide behind caring-sounding emails, or making "sincere" video recordings simply will not do. Giving bad news, is of necessity, a face-to-face business. Doing it well takes practice.

It is not counter-intuitive or rocket science. But it does take emotional intelligence, which appears to be a commodity in rather short supply in some circles.

The first set of decisions to be made is who give the news, to whom and where. Ideally in private and in persona, but who is the best "persona" to do it? Don't treat this as a "let-out" clause, farming the business out to a supportive and empathic subordinate. It is an important issue. Some people have the power, authority and responsibility to give the news.

How many people should be on the giving side and how many on the receiving? It is not meant to be two deputations coming together (à la trade-union bargaining). Yet sometimes recipients feel better if they can bring a friend, a supporter – but hopefully not a lawyer. Usually one-on-one is best. Managers need to prepare how to phrase the crucial bits of the message. One needs mentally to rehearse this. And again the temptation to be vague and pusillanimous is often overwhelming. It is usually not a good idea to have too many "pleasantries" at the beginning. And it is not a good idea to use polite, obfuscating euphemisms. "Gardening leave", "letting go", "outplacement counselling", "consensual exiting" and the like may not be heard as clearly as "I am making you redundant".

After a quick start when it is clear that one is trying to communicate clearly, compassionately and confidentially, it is wise to find out where the employee is "coming from". Few people are ignorant or unaware of serious organizational issues around them. Many suspect what is going to occur. Whether it is discipline or redundancy, many have a good idea of what the meeting is all about.

Breaking bad news is as much about careful listening as careful talking. Best find out early both what they know and what they want to know. Then tell them clearly the central message, the bottom line: "We are making

your position redundant"; "Your promotion application has been unsuccessful"; "You failed the assessment-center test".

Then be prepared for an emotional display. Allow for the message to
sink in – in short, shut up. Variety of responses may occur, from anxiety
and anger, to relief at having been told what they long suspected. The usual
pattern is stunned silence; then tears; then anger, then bargaining. The sto-
ical and repressed may either do or say nothing and save up their outbursts
for a more private moment. The tears bit may be rather embarrassing for
the British male but not that difficult to cope with. Silence, a comforting
touch, an understanding vocalization.

Anger is common – why me; it's so unfair; you and your company are
a bunch of—; I will consult my lawyer/union/journalist friends . . . . It's
easy to react too much to this by being argumentative or combative. And
it's hard to recall that it's a pretty natural response to being hurt, frustrated
or surprised.

Let the cloud burst. Go at their pace. Let them describe fully their feelings. Lance the boil, better now than later. The hard bit is remaining
empathic, patient, understanding. It is this bit people don't like. Yet it may
be the most important part of the whole thing.

It is terribly important to establish what the recipient has heard. It's not
always easy to find that out in a very emotional person. The questions is,
have they heard the message clearly? Do they fully understand what you
are saying? Do they understand the implication?

They may have questions. These need to be anticipated. It might
indeed be a good idea to prepare a short handout with typical questions
and clear responses. Old hands at the business become well versed in
anticipating and answering all the questions, however trivial and daft they
first appear to be.

Best to end by checking their understanding. Perhaps ask them to sum-
marize the central features of the news, as well as, if they want to, their
reactions to them. This offers an opportunity to correct misunderstandings
which can easily occur among all the emotional stuff.

And two other things. Arrange for a follow-up meeting which can go
over the ground. Also take care of your own needs. Don't do these back to
back. It's tiring emotional labor giving bad news and one needs to restore
equilibrium before doing it again without being jaded and inattentive.

The bright boss

It pays to be bright! Intelligence is linked to job performance. Reviews have shown that IQ is also linked to employment record, economic self-sufficiency, affluence, educational achievement as well as marital stability and lawful behavior.

When people are asked what characteristics leaders should have, they always say (amongst other things, like, integrity) "intelligence" or synonyms such as "understanding complex issues".

A recent review of the research published in the 2004 *Journal of Applied Psychology* set out to test various propositions. These included: intelligent people emerge as leaders earlier and more often; intelligence causes a leader to appear leader-like; intelligence is related to leadership better when the leader is not stressed; participative rather than directive leaders are seen as less intelligent.

Results show what one might well suspect. Intelligence is modestly but significantly and positively related to leadership – that is, people prefer bright individuals as leaders. But the more intelligent the leader the more effective is the group on both objective and subjective measures.

Why is this the case? Probably because leadership is about making decisions; collecting, evaluating and weighing up options; tumbling numbers, and so on. Bright people see patterns, connections and trends faster than less bright people.

Bright people also learn faster and more efficiently. In this very fast changing world speed of learning must count for a great deal. And with intelligence probably comes confidence: confidence in one's abilities. Confidence in a leader is not just attractive, it is essential. People whose intelligence means that they have done well in the past are usually confident about doing so again. They are prepared to take (well thought-through) risks. They are happy to try to do things differently.

Leaders have two related types of intelligence – the former leads to the latter. Psychologists distinguish between *fluid* intelligence (the native wit or intelligence to solve new, unfamiliar problems) and *crystallized* intelligence, which is accumulated general knowledge. Both are important. The former dictates the ability to navigate new computer programs; the latter to do crosswords.

Brighter people tend to be better at all tasks. The "multiple intelligence" idea just does not stack up in the empirical literature. Brighter people are good with words and numbers. Brighter people tend to know more.

Being bright is also sexy. Women often use GSOH (good sense of humor) as a code to mean both intellectually and emotionally bright.

But it was most interesting that intelligence was more related to leadership when people were not under stress. The question is when, why and how do people, especially leaders, suffer from stress?

We know that personality and intelligence are not very closely related. Therefore stress proneness (or neuroticism if one dare use the old word) is not associated with big or little intellects. There are bright and dim neurotics. But what the studies do show is that you need to be stable because stress can undo the benefit of your intelligence.

It is of little use being bright if you are anxious, prone to depression or hypochondriachal. You need to be resilient and hardy *and* bright to be a good leader.

.And there is one other finding of interest. The leadership–intelligence link showed up only under directive leaders. Maybe this is pretty obvious – the power, indeed purpose, of a non-directive leader is such that they have relatively little influence.

It does not matter therefore in very democratic, non-directive, situations how bright the leader is. But where they are making regular, relevant, salient day-to-day decisions, it sure counts.

However, it may be less useful, even dysfunctional, if a leader's intelligence substantially exceeds that of the group. The leader may then become easily misunderstood or deeply threatening. So we get the leaders we deserve and understand.

To many, except perhaps the naive, politically correct, or social-equality fans, leaders do better if they are bright. Bright people are seen as more leader-like, get voted more often as leaders and they do a better job once elected. But only if they are stable and directive.

Being bright is not enough. Sure we need emotional intelligence (social skills) and a balanced temperament. But it is difficult to compensate for not being bright enough. The hard-working, non-delegating, slow-to-click managers never quite make it to the top.

Casuistry, sophistry and spin

Casuistry: The false application of general principles to particular instances, especially with regard to morals or law.

Sophistry: Seemingly true but falsely subtle reassuring argumentation.

Spin: To draw out of and twist; to plunge helplessly out of control; to deviate from a straight line.

Jesuits are famous (at least from a Protestant perspective) for their casuistry, lawyers for their sophistry and politicians for their spin. They are all, one way or another, in the same business: the business of persuasion and of conversion. They want your mind, your soul, your vote and often your wallet.

It is no accident that there are so many lawyers and teachers in parliament. Their skills transfer nicely from one job to the other. They are the skills of oratory, of rhetoric and of "believability".

There are media people in parliament. And certainly politicians are very highly media-conscious, to the point often of paranoia. They at once crave, fear and despise the media which oxygenates their world.

But there are two essential differences in the roles and skills that people may want to transfer. The first is the distinction between script generation and script delivery. This is about who pens and who speaks the memorable phrases. Some do both (the multi-skilled), but many more have specialist skills. Hence the brilliant scriptwriter who coins the catchy soundbite, the metaphor that captures the zeitgeist, the slogan which portrays the product.

They need the ear of a poet, the vocabulary of the OED, and the understanding of their audience. They can, like the words of Churchill and Kennedy, capture a historical period for all time.

And some like brilliant actors can deliver lines to make them sing. It can be profoundly disappointing to hear poets read out their own poetry. The poems somehow lose their resonance, their timbre, their very essence. By contrast, they can come alive in the larynx of a drama-schooled trained actor.

Some script, others speak; some do both equally well but they are indeed rarity. Hence the natural writer has to undergo presentation-skills courses. And the natural presenter needs to be helped to choose and use more words, more thoughtfully. Often one finds a happy team where a scriptwriter and a presenter are made for each other. The former can some-how capture the natural tone and rhythm of the latter.

But there is a second, equally important, distinction in this game. It is between the propagandist and the inquisitor, the seller and the buyer, the persuader and the doubter. Everybody has to learn to present a case; they have a mind to shareholders and customers, senior and junior staff as well as the general public. They have to steer a judicious path across a minefield or worse the shifting quicksand of uncertainty, skepticism, and division.

They have always to give the illusion of optimism and control, of both more public services but lower taxes, of higher quality at a cheaper price. This is where a fine appreciation of casuistry, sophistry and spin occurs. This is partly the world of the school debate, the cheap-red-wine-soaked student arguments and, dare one mention it, rows with partners and friends at grown-up dinner parties.

Rhetoricians know that there is a style and a content to persuasive arguments both of which are extremely important. The most unpalatable dish can be served up to look appetizing. There is a time, a place and a way both to hide and to present bad news. Whether it be proof of the existence of God (or aliens), the future of heavy industry or the viability of socia-lism, these ideas (messages) can be well packaged.

But at least in the antiphonal world of the BBC, for every propagandist there is an inquisitor. These are the balloon deflators, the saberd incisors, the pomposity prickers of the law, the media and the angry shareholders. They have been also trained in the philosophical art of logical analysis.

Their job is to expose false logic, hypocrisy, ambiguity and the like. They have to be the fearless David against the often important and seem-ingly omnipotent Goliath. Their task is to cross-examine then steal back the conch shell from the person who is zealously gripping it. Their *raison d'être* is to ensure that the powerful are truly understood by their constituency.

Propagandists and inquisitors, like speech writers and deliverers, are different people. The propagandist may have traits better suited to that black art than those of an inquisitor. But the best can do both. In this sense one can and should be both defense and prosecution lawyer. One has really to know, practice and have used the tricks of the trade to be able to detect and challenge them.

Choosing management courses

Management education is big business. There are now nearly a hundred university-based business schools in Britain alone, all eager to attract high-fee-paying MBA students.

There are also dozens of short courses, seminars, conferences, breakfast meetings, symposia and the like, aimed at the lucrative management-training sector.

Most senior people, in both private and public sector, are "junk-mailed," it seems almost daily, to attend crucially important, state-of-the-art courses. Organizations often have a generous training budget, particularly in good times. So courses mushroom to fill the perceived need.

But how can individuals and organizations ensure they choose wisely? How to be sure you get value for money? How to sift the wheat from the chaff; the exaggerated promise from the often disappointing reality?

One assessment-center exercise asked candidates to describe what they would do with a £5000 cheque and a month off work to improve their skills and productivity. It involved deciding what knowledge or skills are required (self-diagnosis); selecting how, when, and where to acquire them (choose the best courses); and how to both implement and retain the skills (evaluate course success).

It was a good exercise. Some wags maintained that what they needed was a rest/sabbatical and would gain as much sailing around the Med or attending a very expensive wine-tasting course in Bordeaux as going to a posh business school.

Examiners were interested in which skills or knowledge the candidates argued they needed. Were they realistic and insightful or just showing off? What was their rationale for the type of courses they chose? What evidence did they have that it delivered what they wanted? Precisely how would it benefit them, or help them at work? How could the employer know it was good value for money? Was there an over- or underspend?

Choosing a good course is a difficult business. Most people work on about three factors: reputation, personal recommendation and price. These are quite insufficient as criteria. People and institutions often have reputations they do not deserve. It takes a long time to gain a good reputation but rather less time to lose it. This benefits older, better-established institutions which may be resting on their laurels or their marketing spin.

Equally, individuals may have reputations quite out of line with their ability to teach. People who write good books may not be able to instruct or enthuse well. People who appear on the television a lot may do a brilliant soundbite or ask tough questions but can they sustain a day-long training session? Motivational speakers can't often do more than an hour or so and the "feel good factor" soon wears off. Entertainers get great feedback, but people learn very little in their courses as they are aimed precisely at feedback sheets, not real learning.

Personal recommendation seems sensible as long as you can separate content and style. There are radical differences in how individuals like to teach and learn. Some like the MBA-styled high interaction method based on case studies. Others prefer the formal lecture that starts with theory and evidence. Still others like "learning by doing" or observing in the "shadowing" sense. Certainly what is taught is relevant to the teaching method but what a friend enjoyed or benefited from may not benefit you.

You need to make sure that a recommender has the same motives, needs, and level of experience as you before following their advice. And never forget the power of dissonance or "buyers nostalgia", which means that in order to justify the expenditure of great amounts of time and (usually) other people's money, employees feel obliged to paint a very rosy picture of the course they attended.

And price is also a poor criterion. Price is usually determined by what the market can stand, not the value of the course. There are many constraints that need to be taken into consideration, such as the cost of buildings, staff and so on which have little relationship to the content of the course.

Lecturers have noticed that course evaluation is as much a function of the quality of accommodation and meals as the educational bit. They also know that the quantity of handouts and the contents of the "party bag" leaving the course (few books, pens, and so on) are really important.

So, if reputation, recommendation and price are insufficient, what should you look for? There are at least half a dozen relevant criteria:

1. *Staff:* Who is teaching on this course? What are their educational and experiential qualifications? There are many management teachers or gurus who have one sort of experience but not the other, highly published dons who have never managed anything or anybody, or early-retired managers eager to improve their pension, or who find teaching less stressful than actually managing. The former know the theory, the latter the practice.

2. *Educational philosophy:* Is it examined? What is the post-course follow-up? What is the balance between individual and groupwork and why? Has the course changed much in the past and why? What is the mix of educational methods: video, seminar, case study?

3. *Skills vs knowledge:* Is the course essentially about learning about something or how to do something, or both? If it is skills learning, how are they best taught?

4. *Massed vs distributed learning:* We know that if a course lasts for five days it is educationally better to have five Mondays in a row than Monday to Friday one week. People learn better and more efficiently when they have homework exercises between course parts/modules.

5. *Course attendees:* People attend courses to network. Many say they learn as much from others on the course as their teachers. Everyone has experience of the great course because of the quality of other delegates: their ability, experience, desire to have fun, contribution and so on. So we need reassurance about the quality and number of the other participants.

6. *Possibility of follow-up:* What happens after the course? Does it lead to anything specific? Is there an advanced course? How can you make sure the learning is retained and practiced?

7. *Recognition:* Is the course recognized as worthwhile by a professional body, by your industry, or your organization?

Some very expensive courses have a simple formula. First, make sure that accommodation, meals and so on are first class. Next, wheel in a few world-famous lecturers. Three, make candidates work very hard with difficult assignments and case studies to prove that they both need education and are lacking in skills. Next, encourage the students to bond and to share their experience. Finally, pass everybody, give them fancy certificates and enrol them in the alumni association. That is, treat them as real graduates even if they have only been on a three-week course. And, if you are shrewd, have some reunions as well as the advanced course.

Compulsory training

Should companies be compelled to spend money on training? Should they be encouraged and exhorted to invest in their people? Should they be taxed if they do not or receive rebates and subsidies if they do?

Governments appear equivocal on this issue. Few doubt some worrying statistics. A frighteningly large number of the British workforce (a fifth) are considered to be functionally illiterate. Some believe that as many as half the British workforce have the numeracy skills expected of an eleven-year-old. And we have a comparative skills deficit.

But worse, skills and their deficit are directly, linearly and logically linked to expansion, investment and productivity. To maintain a healthy, vibrant economy we need a skilled, and continuously re-upskilling work-force. We therefore get a good return on investment in training. It is not an option but a necessity.

This "logic" however begs three very big questions. *First*, who should pay for the training? *Second*, precisely what training, for whom to what end? *Third*, what is the evidence that training works, that is, what evidence of real ROI, wherever the money comes from?

First, who should pay? The companies who are the immediate benefi-ciaries or the government? Most governments pursue a voluntary approach. Companies are neither (financially) rewarded nor punished for investing in any sort of training. And, say many, so it should be.

Organizations say it is the education system, not them, that is failing. Why should they pick up the prices and the tab? It is the government-run education system which should ensure that those who leave school are properly educated. To coerce private industry to do what government has failed to do is hypocritical, to say the least.

Further, if there were a clear ROI on training, all (successful) compa-nies would train their employees anyway. All organizations try to recruit, select and retain the best, and help them stay that way. Trust organizations to do just that: all this flim flam about training is a huge waste of public money, a charter for training expansion not skills expansion.

What those in favor of (compulsory) training say is this. Companies audit their workforce skill set and the gap between what is required/ideal and what actually exists. Next they plan, administer and evaluate training dedicated to filling that gap. To be recognized, this process should be transparent, public and open to scrutiny.

Over time, there have been various government initiatives to encourage training. We had the Modern Apprenticeship Scheme, the National Vocational Qualification (some say *Not Very Qualified*) idea and, more recently, Investors in People. We have had Training and Enterprise Councils and proposals for a National Skills Agenda.

The questions from all this effort and industry are manifold. Given that (so far) everything is (ultimately) voluntary there are questions of *adoption*. Next what is the impact on training activity, company morale, and so on? But perhaps most important of all, what is the (actual, real, sustained) impact on business performance? That is, is there any relationship between training activity and performance measures? If so, is it direct or indirect (through employee attitude, flexibility)? And is it tangible and measurable, or intangible and not measurable? Do we have to take everything on trust? Is it all a matter of faith?

Simple big questions call for simple big answers. The trouble is things are (inevitably) a bit more complicated. What skills are we talking about: hard (technical) or soft (people-oriented)? Are the skills highly task-specific or transferable? More important, what types of training work best? Lots of short courses or one long course? Training at work or off-site? Specialist trainers or selected managers?

How often does training need to be "topped up"? Are some people better trainers and trainees than others? Is the link between training activity and business need always retrospective and therefore always (paradoxically) too late? Is experiential "soft" developmental learning better than task-oriented, formalized, prescriptive training? Hard is easier to measure. Soft is more important.

Lots of ifs and buts. Lots of ways to prove one's case either way. Coercion may mean organizations will always chase badge-collecting, plaque-displaying, guru-led training fads. Others will always cast doubt on the ROI of such things, preferring either to select their skills base (rather than train it) and endorse an apprenticeship, mentoring model.

But whoever is to blame and whoever's responsibility it is, it seems very difficult to believe we can be complacent about the general skills level of our current workforce.

Correcting cock-ups

Everyday and in every way cock-ups occur in business. Unplanned, unforeseen and certainly undesirable, they can upset staff, customers and assorted victims in a big way. Machinery breaks down, absenteeism causes staff shortages, mistakes of all sorts occur. It's all part of growing up and being human.

But what distinguishes different organizations is how they deal with problems. What are staff instructed or empowered to do when a failure in delivery occurs?

There are two clear extremes: deniers and recoverers. The former are probably the most common. They come in various forms, from the total to the partial. Deniers have an "act of God" philosophy. So there was a cock-up – that's life. They believe three fundamental things, only the *first* of which is true. They know that accidents, errors and mistakes occur, sometimes too frequently and for all sorts of reasons. *Second,* they believe that the majority of complainants are lying, litigious louts, who were either the cause of the problem themselves or vastly exaggerated the consequences for others. They believe that these people are on the make, rapidly increasing in number, and a serious threat to the profitability (even existence) of their organization and the whole enterprise.

Third, they believe the best way to cope with this cancer, this menace, this virus is to stand firm. Standing firm involves a number of stages like retreat lines on a battlefield. *First* deny there is anything wrong. Bluff and ignore. Certainly don't have a complaints desk or call line. Or if you do, man it sporadically. Next, if that fails, blame the complainant for causing the problem.

The *second* stage can really inflame the pissed-off complainant and if they know their rights and how to exercise them – beware. This is not the "write to consumer magazine" school of letter-writing and complaint but the "contact the CEO, the analysts and the media" approach.

The *third* stage is not to admit fault, but to make some paltry offer to placate the complainant: a miserable sum of money; another ticket to the show; a voucher unlikely to be redeemed. Again this has the power to enrage as much as to placate.

Most people want the issue fixed: another flight or meal; their money refunded in full; a working model replacing the broken one. *And* they want a polite apology. Resourceful adults and enraged complainants usually hold out to the end. Further, they have discovered that there are numerous television and radio programmes eager to hear their story. They have also found the shareholders meeting an excellent place to embarrass a lot of people.

Throughout this protracted enterprise complainers act as brand terrorists, telling their story again and again and making others doubt the value of the brand. Whether they succeed or not in extracting an apology and/or compensation they all swear (time and again) and as publicly as possible never to use the organization again.

Deniers differ in how long they are prepared to hold out and how much they give in the end. And the effects are proportional.

The other extreme has quite a different philosophy. They also know that cock-ups occur. And they are also not unaware that some people make false complaints, or grossly exaggerated complaints. But they do know a few things. And they are backed-up by various Harvard Business School studies.

They know one fundamental, perhaps surprising fact. It is this: people often feel better disposed to an organization after an error has been corrected than if the error did not occur in the first place. Customers see these organizations as caring, considerate and kind. They can become more, rather than less brand loyal.

So the best organizations empower their staff at the lowliest customer-facing level to make decisions and compensate. Waiters can give free bottles of wine, dry-cleaning vouchers and complimentary dishes. Bank staff can simply cancel charges. Flight crew can sign promissory letters.

And really big organizations set up centers dedicated to customer recovery. Sure, there are a few shysters. But it's cost effective, possibly very much more so, to let a few of these through the net than anger and alienate the genuine.

And whereas denial leads to brand terrorists, so recovery leads to apostles for the brand. A happy bunny, a happy camper is a good broadcaster for the brand.

The curse of perfectionism

A highly desirable trait that ensures high standards, quality assurance and utter reliability or a psychological handicap indicative of dithering, delay and delusions? Healthy drive or self-destructive perfectionism?

The concept of the perfectionist can be both positive and negative. There is the idea of the nit-picker – someone who looks for the hole in a transparent window. But we talk about the perfect holiday, the perfect meal and cry with delight "Sheer perfection". Surely then, those who seek to produce it in the kitchen or factory, studio or office are admirable people?

Perfectionists value and foster excellence and they strive to meet important goals. In certain areas like sports and science, perfectionism is not just tolerated but encouraged. To some, perfectionism is about high standards, persistence, conscientiousness. Perfectionists are organized. They have self-imposed high standards and in the role of parent, teacher or mentor, tend to impose those high standards on others. Combined with ability and stability, perfectionists can, should and do, reach their ultimate level of performance.

But note the term stability. There is a dark side to perfectionism. It is seen as a cause and correlate of serious psychopathology. At worst, perfectionists believe they should be perfect: no hesitations, deviations or inconsistencies. They are super-sensitive to imperfection, failing, weakness. And they believe their acceptance and lovability is a function of never making mistakes. They don't know the meaning of "good enough". All or nothing . . . .

Psychologists see the trait of perfectionism almost always as a handicap. They see perfectionists as vulnerable to distress, often haunted by a chronic sense of failure, indecisiveness and its close companion procrastination, and also shame.

The clinical-take on perfectionism is that it can and does involve setting excessively high personal standards and stringently evaluating one's behavior in light of them. It can also mean imposing one's standards on others and having equally high (often quite unrealistic) expectations of them. Perfectionists often believe that powerful others (bosses, parents, spouses) expect one to be perfect (in all ways) and are harsh, punitive, unforgiving judges. Perfectionists are rigid.

So where does perfectionism come from? Parents, of course. As always. They may be critical and demanding. Perfectionists in adulthood live with their parents' voice and their standards. The way psychologists measure perfectionism probably explains best how they conceive of it. Measurement is mainly done by questionnaire or interview. And tests are multi-dimensional, trying to capture the full range of issues.

One issue is *concern over mistakes* which reflects negative reactions to mistakes, a tendency to interpret mistakes as equivalent to failure, and a tendency to believe that one will lose the respect of others following failure ("People will probably think less of me if I make a mistake"; "I should be upset if I make a mistake"). A second issue is of *personal standards* which reflect the setting of very high standards and the importance placed on these high standards for self-evaluation ("If I do not set the highest standards for myself, I am likely to end up a second-rate person"; "I hate being less than the best at things"). The tendency to believe that one's parents set very high goals comprises the third issue of *parental expectations* ("My parents expected excellence from me"; "My parents wanted me to be the best at everything"). Fourthly, the perception that one's parents are (or were) overly critical constitutes the *parental criticism* ("As a child I was punished for doing things less than perfect"; "I never felt like I could meet my parents' standards"). Another feature is the *doubting of actions,* which reflects the extent to which people doubt their ability to accomplish tasks. Finally, excessive importance can be placed on *order and organization* ("Organization is very important to me"; "I try to be a neat person").

So pity the poor perfectionist. They are driven by a fear of failure: a fear of making mistakes, a fear of disapproval. They can easily self-destruct in a vicious cycle of their own making. Set unreachable goals → fail to reach them → become depressed and lethargic → have less energy, with a deep sense of failure → get lower self-esteem and high self-blame.

Pathological perfectionists are both unhappy and unproductive. They tend to have low self-esteem because they feel they are losers. And there is always the ghost of guilt and its fellow-travelers of shame and self-recrimination. Most perfectionists struggle with depression, pessimism and low self-belief. They can easily become immobilized and be without motivation. But when they are at it perfectionists are marked by their compulsivity, obsessionality and rigidity.

Perfectionists, poor souls, need help. Nothing wrong with setting high standards, but they need to be reachable with effort. It's all about being OK, human not super-human, among the best, if not the best.

Perfectionism can be a curse. Perfectionists are carriers of criticism both of self and others. And by setting standards at the wrong level they are condemned never to achieve them.

amned if you do and . . . don't

Compensation claims and "ambulance chasing" lawyers have made the business of selection a nightmare. In America, the bottom has fallen out of the intelligence-testing market as a result of actual or threatened lawsuits, because they apparently discriminate against blacks.

Recruiters and selectors, even trainees, have had to become aware of the impact both of legislation and of political correctness on many tests. Tests of abilities and attitudes, of personality and preferences, of vocational choices and values, all apparently have to pass various screens to ensure they do not discriminate against women (or men), the handicapped; the aged, non-English speaking people, and so on.

The theory is that tests of many kinds may discriminate all right, not only between potentially good and bad employees but also on other grounds which is unfair, unwise and illegal. Despite pretty minimal evidence on the topic the anti-test movement has gained sway and now selectors are wary.

Without tests (of any type), selectors and screeners revert to the famous trio: the application form, the interview and the references. However both the former and the latter have been under the scrutiny of the politically correct police and lawyers and thus yield far less information. There is now a variety of things you can't or shouldn't ask on forms: age, health history, and so on. Some would argue that application forms have become thus worthless in selection, because the most useful, potentially diagnostic and differentiating information cannot be asked.

The same is true of references. Again because of legal suits, some businesses will only confirm that a former employee worked from date A to date B. Nothing is to be said about their work performance over this period, or indeed why they left.

So the interview has to be the source of everything. And this is where the problem is. Consider some more specialist jobs, those whose job involves risk: police who carry firearms; detectives in specialist fraud or pornography; those who screen others at airports; those who deal in secrets. How do you select reliable employees and screen out the bad apples?

So what next? An obvious answer: sue those who make poor selection decisions, who got it wrong, perhaps indeed through failing to use a test.

The Roman Catholic Church knows all about this. Cardinals, bishops and the like are all under the microscope for not selecting out and/or dealing with known pedophiles. The sin is that of selection: not spotting that an ordinand was potentially sexually compromised.

The question is how to get at the dark side of an applicant's personality. Psychiatrists would call them "personality disorders" laypeople "derailers". It means finding cold, callous, amoral individuals who have a history of lying, stealing and cheating. There are other types however, equally likely to cause mayhem in a business. These include those with narcissistic, paranoid or schizoid disorders.

There are now valid tests and checklists which can help selectors find these individuals. The clever, good-looking psychopath is a potential wrecker of all businesses. They are hard to spot, brilliant at charm and weaving a completely believable story. Narcissists have wonderful self-confidence, again thought to be attractive. The paranoid seem attractive to organizations that themselves have more than a touch of that world-view.

One consultant recently remarked to a client "Give me the money now; or give it to me later". What he meant was "Let me use valid and reliable and proven tests for selection at the beginning, or pay me in coaching, outplacement or remedial training once the inevitable problems have been detected".

Testing is not a panacea. It simply helps, like all other data sets, to improve decision-making. All selectors should be in the business of selecting in and selecting out. You choose the right, eliminate the wrong. And now you can be sued for both selecting and rejecting, whereas in the past rejections were rarely a source of litigation. Select someone who abuses children; select someone who fails to detect bombs; select someone who is an imposter; select someone who sabotages a plant; select someone who embezzles the company . . . and you could be sued by the victims of the misdemeanor. You missed a trick and placed people in danger.

It may be, however, that your problem with selection is not the legal issue: far worse than that, you may be systematically selecting people who through their indolence, sloth and negativity simply grind the company down until it fails. And in this instance the selector becomes the selected.

Damned if you do, and damned if you don't. The money now or the money later. Sued for errors of commission; sued for errors of omission. The moral of the story: decision-making has its costs. And they are getting higher. Gut feelings, common sense and "years of experience" are no substitute for good data. Psychopaths, pedophiles and others are very difficult to detect. It is worth the investment and risk of spending money up front not just to cover your back but to make better choices.

Dom and sub

Dominance and submission are terms rarely found in management tomes. They are more likely to be found in curiously opposite texts: the erotic, pleasure-seeking world of sexual preferences and perversions and the cold, controlling world of religious practice and faith. Or, perhaps in describing well-suited but maladjusted types. The odd couple; the codependent; the sickly suited. Neither dom nor sub are good words. They are, quite simply, not "polite" concepts.

But they are at the heart of business. Go to a board meeting and watch! And the increasing cases of bullying is usually about either a manager not knowing how to dominate and/or an employee unwilling to submit.

And yet any observer of their domestic pet sees, on a daily basis, the interplay of dominance and submission. In the animal world, dominance and leadership are almost, it seems, interchangeable concepts.

Animals, especially primates, but most mammals and everything from chickens to lizards, establish their power, leadership and authority by aggressive dominance. The alpha male has choice over the females by his aggressive display of force, strength and will.

A pet enthusiast, be they pigeon or piscine fanciers, terrier breeders or tortoise keepers often try to breed dominance in their pets. It is no accident that tattooed, aggressive young men choose rottweilers and other bull-terrier breeds or crossbreeds to emphasize or enhance their masculinity, their aggressiveness and their (anti) social dominance.

Some dog breeds seem to scream "Don't mess with me, I am top dog". Others specialize in submission, often to a human looking for a child substitute. Killer dogs and lap-dog poodles.

But dominance is also a social and a comparative concept. Social animals form into flat, but distinct hierarchies with three to four levels: the alpha male or the matriarch, the senior wives, the junior wives and the near-adolescents.

But you don't have to go on safari to see dominance. Kindergartens have all the data you need. Observe a group of four-year-olds. Some steal toys and attention: they get what they want more by force than charm. They bully, threaten and take what they want. Others get what they want by early forms of charm and assertiveness. They disarm by directness but not of a threatening nature.

And this is the beginning of two forms of dominance – pro- and anti-aggression. So where does dominance come from? As always, a mixture of nature and nurture. Parents are, of course, to blame in the nurture bit. Those who major on authoritarianism, rules and restrictions can encourage either strong dominance or submission, depending on the temperament of the child. It has long been known that the bully and the bullied often share various psychological characteristics. Neither is assertive. Those who prefer authoritativeness, warmth and reason breed compliant but appropriately assertive, children. There are, in short, healthy and unhealthy parental styles.

By the time they reach the age of work, adults appear to have a well-developed capacity for dominance and status-seeking. Getting ahead, being promoted, having a big staff under you is very desirable and admirable.

Some have this need more strongly – others do not. But if you do not have powerful "dominance need" genes, it does not necessarily follow that you are submissive. You may simply conform to the role. After all one needs to know when to be a follower and when a leader.

The army believes you have to learn to be a good follower before you can become an effective leader. And they certainly know about "dom 'n' sub". You have to know how and when to take orders (unquestioningly) and equally when to give them. The whole system works on this principle and rather well. All armies follow the same formula and have for thousands of years.

People learn to conform, submit to the roles, rules and other requirements of the organization. They have to learn to be reasonable, reliable and responsible.

There are more acceptable psychological and "business speak" words for dom and sub. These include striving for superiority, status-seeking, need for power.

But in the adult business world, dominance and submission are not antonymous concepts. As soon as you translate the concepts into "status striving" and "conformity", then it is clear. It's a matter of knowing what is required and when. Sort of business etiquette.

Dominance is related to robust, rigoros leadership; submission to being rated as someone with potential. The two go hand in hand. Those who can't swap roles never get on, because they do not understand when to give and when to take orders.

Energy at work

Energy is a hot topic. Whether it be the energy that powers our cars and computers or physical energy to remain alert, active and attentive at the end of the day.

There are manifold political issues with respect to energy, from those who hound 4 × 4 drivers to the "good-life greenies" eager to recycle and reduce waste. Workplaces are often temples of waste particularly paper, heat and food. Some nod in the direction of the "waste police", with paper recycling, stamp collecting, toner recycling, even food collection for shelters.

But personal energy is equally important. And there may be two interlinked personal energy systems. The first is physical. Older people have less energy than younger people. Sick people have less energy than well people. Sleep-deprived people are less energetic than the well-rested.

The second is psychological energy. This has been conceived of in different ways. The Freudians conceived a psychic energy: a vital, cryptosexual force, that drives us to want and do things we barely understand. Thus we can be driven to arational, irrational, downright bizarre behaviors because of these unconscious libidinos springs. The Freudians stick to Victorian engineering metaphors with all their pipes, pistons and steam.

For the Freudians there are three powerful forces: the *ego* or self; the *superego* or conscience and the *id* or instincts. These three are in constant combat: the id demands immediate immoral gratification, the superego says "No"; the ego tries to be rational. As one psychologist once memorably put it, "Personality is a battlefield". A sex-crazed monkey (the id) is forever engaged in mortal combat in a dark cellar with a well-bred spinster lady (the superego), refereed by a rather nervous bank clerk (the ego). So the pleasure principle is the accelerator, the conscience the brake and the reality principle the steering wheel of life.

Dark, powerful energetic forces bubble up from the volcano of the unconscious, emerging somewhat differently in the conscious mind.

But you don't have to be a Freudian to appreciate energy at work. Personality factors are also related to energy. Extraverts appear more (socially) energetic but burn up easily with their impulsivity and impatience. Introverts have a much slower burning fuse and are able to sustain longer periods of attentiveness under conditions of poor arousal.

Neurotics waste their energy. They burn it up on the irrelevant and the imaginary. They can easily become anxious, then depressed, by small things.

They fritter away their additional nervous energy rather than conserve it for the long haul or the really important. Paradoxically then, they appear to have more energy than their stable opposites but waste it on worry. And they end up exhausted.

And intelligence is a driving force. The bright have more intellectual energy: more curiosity, more openness-to-new-experience. They use their energy more efficiently. Indeed one definition of intelligence is about energy efficient brain processing.

Work is tiring, be it physical or mental, or some combination of the two. Productive and satisfied workers need enough energy and they need to know how to expend it wisely.

Job advertisements, especially those aimed at recruiting young graduates for highly pressurized (usually City but also Public Sector) positions, sometimes speak of "high-energy individuals". They might as well add impervious to sleep deprivation and the effects of "weekend working" to the list of desirable characteristics for these high energy burn-out careers.

Appraisals for the highly remunerated incumbents may rate energy levels directly or indirectly, for example by citing an individual's "recovery time" after meeting a particularly gruelling deadline, or noting absence incurred through jetlag.

In most jobs, energy levels are not referred to explicitly. Instead, a position may be described as "not a 9 to 5 job", or some other euphemism that indicates that the days will be long and energy required high.

Energy level seldom seems to be a recognized competency or attribute, or an explicit criterion for selection.

Engagement to divorce

Relationships go through phases. People meet, explore, date and then become "an item". Their intention to marriage may be made explicit in the charming idea of an engagement with all the trimmings: the announcement in the newspaper, the ring, the engagement party, and the plans for the big day.

The wedding usually follows: expensive, exhausting, possibly exhilarating. And then for an increasing number (well over 30%) separation, divorce and all the psychological stuff that goes with it. A pattern, a cycle. Of course the fairytale does not end in divorce but in marital bliss.

Could this pattern be a useful metaphor for a working life? Can you be engaged or married to an organization? Priests, monks and nuns are married to the Church (through Christ) explicitly. But how is the work contract different from a prenuptial contract?

Gurus have felt the need to use new words to express job satisfaction and worker morale. They appear to have settled on engagement. How useful is this concept? What is its opposite? How and when do you engage people and what happens when they become disengaged?

Engagement is the new word for job satisfaction. It is an index of morale and commitment. It is the opposite of alienation. To be engaged is to be absorbed and attracted. It can mean to engross. It can mean to bind and to mesh.

The engaged worker is the ideal worker. They take their work seriously. It holds their attention. They are always fully involved, fully occupied. Many are intrinsically satisfied and motivated. They experience "flow" at work. Their absorption makes time fly. And the reward is the activity itself.

A couple's engagement party is a significant event. It is a celebration of a pledge. It is a public announcement of a promise that symbolizes an emotional state.

So why not have engagement parties at work? You could also have re-engagement parties. And perhaps disengagement wakes.

A work-based engagement party could be for those staff who demonstrate all the criteria of engagement to the organization. It would celebrate their happy state.

And equally one may mark a separation and even perhaps a divorce. "Separation" is usually cessation of cohabitation. This may start with separate beds, then separate rooms, then separate houses and separate lives. But it begins with an emotional separation.

Some people at work are separated. Their bonds and bands have been broken. They no longer love nor care much about their work or the welfare of the company. They are the disengaged. Work is a dreary drag, a tedious necessity, a boring interlude.

They are completely extrinsically oriented. They are there only for the comp and ben; the salary, the pension and the share options.

Perhaps naming and shaming the disengaged might start with disengagement wakes. Here the managers lament the passing of a colleague from the happy state of engagement to the much less happy state they are in. There could be a few good rituals symbolizing their enthusiasm being snuffed out.

And then there are divorce parties when employers celebrate the sacking of a lazy, incompetent, abusive or bullying colleague.

They say we don't celebrate things enough at work. Perhaps we should see the career in traditional relationship terms with the christening party on arrival; the engagement party when one is doing really well; the disengagement wake as a wake-up call to shape up or ship out and the divorce (with alimony) when it's finally over.

Evangelists at work

Exactly two hundred years ago a German polymath wrote a couple of papers in an academic journal on a topic that still provokes passionate debate. His thesis, the antithetical antecedent of Karl Marx was that religious beliefs, not economic forces or the class struggle, lead to wealth creation.

He developed the notion of the Protestant work ethic: the idea that the beliefs and values and subsequent behaviors of the Protestants of Europe, as compared to the Catholics, directly led to their national wealth increasing.

Weber identified various features of the wealth-creating belief system. First that all work, however menial, is ultimately for God's glory. Idleness is wasteful and sinful. Next there was the radical idea that wealth is a sign of God's grace. The fruits of one's labor are manifest in accumulating wealth. The chosen have lots of (honestly earned) dosh and the poor (at least the indolent and undeserving) are the damned. Radical stuff, particularly today.

The third corner of this sturdy and powerful edifice was compulsory asceticism: sort of neo-Amish simplicity. Thus, although one was encouraged to accumulate wealth, there were strict rules for spending it. Further investment – good. Conspicuous consumption – bad. Ideal for capitalism: the reinvesting entrepreneur, not the self-indulgent, spendthrift playboy.

And finally the Protestants were urged to be rational and self-sufficient. They rejected the sacramental system of Catholicism with all it hierarchies. Theirs was a simple, just, if stern God, and he could be contacted directly.

According to Weber these beliefs led to business behaviors which saw capitalism flourish. Order, justice, hard work, self-discipline, and a respect for wealth (and fear of poverty) was the engine that powered parts of Europe, more than others, before and after the industrial revolution.

The energy of religion is being rediscovered, particularly in America. Various groups are eager to harness the potential power and force of religious beliefs and conviction. They have discovered a new intelligence – spiritual intelligence.

What is spiritual intelligence and why is it important? Apparently it has something to do with investing the everyday (work) event with a sense of the sacred or divine. So we see workplace spirituality and spiritual wellness workshops to promote spiritual health and growth.

And guess what? There is supposed to be a (proven or provable) connection between workplace spirituality and all aspects of organizational processes, from motivation to satisfaction and leadership to innovation.

Spiritual employees, it is claimed are differentially motivated and satisfied; they are physically and mentally healthier; they put in fewer claims, steal and cheat less. And spiritual employees become the new, sexy type of "servant leaders". They also find their creative juices are more easily liberated. They are more attuned to work – life balance issues and they form more cohesive teams.

Cynics see this spiritual revival as an attempt to give meaning to alienated, post-materialist people. We are social, but also ideological animals. As we see, to our shock and shame, people are (seemingly happily) prepared to make the ultimate sacrifice for their beliefs. People will kill others and themselves and endure chronic and acute hardship for strongly held beliefs.

Imagine the benefits of harnessing this force at work. Imagine the cost savings and benefits of a workforce happy in the knowledge that their efforts are for God's glory and personal salvation, not just for salaries, holidays and pensions.

Of course, nineteenth-century Protestantism needs to be repackaged. People appear to like a bit of crypto-Catholic mysticism and new-age flummery. They seem to enjoy yearning for a sense of peace and purpose and connection. And meaning.

The concept of the Industrial Chaplain ministering to the needs of exhausted hands in clapped-out factories has been replaced by a more feminine counselling type who brings calm and refreshment.

Everyone is a winner

School sports days and end-of-term prize-giving sessions have changed. There is a pervasive, evidence-free myth that by identifying some individuals as successes, those not so recognized feel depressed.

The argument is that by publicly differentiating the more and the less talented hard-working or ambitious one creates two spirals. The *virtuous circle* means that "to him who hath more shall be given". While the *vicious cycle* means downwards to doom and depression.

The eye of the self-appointed socially concerned counselors naturally alights on the victims of viciousness. They believe that if one does not receive recognition and prizes for ability and effort (however equitable that might be) people lose their self-confidence and self-esteem. This in turn leads them both to try less hard, less often, and even become phobic about competitive situations. So everything is self-fulfilling and it begins with prizes.

They also believe that self-confidence is vital. That confidence leads to performance and not vice versa. So the key is self-esteem – hence the American-led and almost obsessional self-esteem movement. The idea is to nurture and bolster children's self-esteem – especially those who are disadvantaged – so that they might realize their full potential.

So *all* must have prizes at all competitive events. Either they will all get something or no one gets anything. Equality over equity. This philosophy has at least three major and significant problems associated with it. The *first* is that once young people have left the cloistered and protective world of educational and recreational institutions, they find the "real" world is full of cut and thrust, winners and losers, the accepted and the rejected. Not quite dog-eat-dog, but certainly where competition is rejoiced in rather than rejected.

It then comes as a terrible shock to the self-esteem-bolstered young person. Indeed, the President of the American Psychological Society recently suggested that the increase in adolescent suicide may be directly attributable to the "all must have prizes" philosophy. Is not the task of the educators to prepare pupils for the real world, not protect them from it?

The world of work, relationships and recreation is a competitive world. We learn both to cooperate and to compete. And we learn about the benefits of hard work, practice and sacrifice. At the Olympic games only winners get prizes.

The *second* issue is that of direction of causality. This is essentially whether the causal relationship between self-esteem and (academic) performance is from the former to the latter or vice versa. The self-esteem movement insists the former; the doubters, the latter. Self-esteem does influence self-confidence but unless it is, at least partly, related to ability and effort, it is rather hollow.

One could make a good case for "performance leads to performance". All people get a good sense of how they are doing, comparatively over time and with others. They see and feel their development and respond to it. Thus, for the sports coach the target is behavior, skill, performance, not self-esteem. Do well and you feel good about yourself.

Thirdly, there is a yet more worrying consequence of the "all must have prizes" philosophy and it can be clearly seen in our current educational crisis. This refers essentially to the effect on the talented. Concentrating on the processes in the vicious circle ignores the issues of the virtuous cycle. If all get prizes, how does this affect the talented and able?

The A-level crisis and the first-class degree problem is a manifestation of the issue. Whether exams are getting easier, students brighter or lectures and marking more lenient is not the issue. The issue is about differentiation.

Peers know more about ability and effort than teachers. All students know which of their group are really talented or indeed who make up for it by conscientious endeavor. By sending the signal that ability and effort are not that important, because whatever you do you receive a prize, can very fundamentally demoralize the talented. It sends the signal that input is not related to output; that inequality of performance is met with equality of reward.

Some believe the talented and hardworking are robust enough to withstand all this. Others secretly enjoy the *schadenfreude* of it all; how the mighty have fallen. If the system is fair in the sense that real winners are identifiable and identified then paradoxically the "all must have prizes" philosophy can be a double whammy. It does not succeed in raising the performance of the less successful and demotivates the really successful.

All must *not* have prizes!

Family business

In many parts of Asia (India, China) there is a long tradition of the family business. All members of the family are expected to work in the business which they know, one day, will become theirs. They are very common. Perhaps 80% of the world's businesses are family firms. Certainly only just under half of the Fortune 500 companies are family owned and controlled.

For small businesses, from the newsagent to the restaurant, this may be a very sensible and economically wise act. It does however attract criticism of jealous competitors who claim family members either "work" for less than the legal minimum wage or else are exploiting child-labor laws.

Family are supposedly reliable, loyal and trustworthy. They have serious stakes in the outcome of the organization and may be therefore intrinsically motivated. Their foibles, strengths and weaknesses are well understood. It takes the risk out of recruitment and selection. Family members know all about each other's abilities, proclivities, quirks – or they should!

It is, in many ways the royal principle: the dynasty model. For thousands of years in Europe and still in many parts of the world today the "hereditarian" principle prevailed. It seemed the natural order of things. It meant people could safely bequeath their life achievements to those who shared their genes down the generations. Even the Americans liked this. And it is still possible to see someone write "Eugene B Wopenheimer III".

It is also believed by some that family members are ideally suited to take over a business because of both nature and nurture. That is, having inherited genes from parents they (hopefully) have inherited some of the aptitudes and skills required for the business: academic or emotional intelligence, sociability, stability, fortitude and diligence.

But they will also have been socialized and nurtured in the business culture. They will appreciate and understand from a very early age the importance of customer responsiveness, stock depreciation, profit, and so on. Through observation, education and participation they will not only understand the world of business long before their contemporaries but understand it better.

But it is quite a different matter "handing over" or "grooming one's children" to take over the family empire. There are many famous examples where the parent educates their children to take over the job and ownership of the company.

The problems for the concept of the family business lie in many areas. What if there are no children? What if all the children show no aptitude for the business? What if they show aptitudes to work in a completely different business sector? What if there is a squabble, tussle between family members who both/all want to take over the business? What if the chosen successor openly and explicitly disagrees how the business is doing and wants to take it in a very different direction?

Many self-made business people find it difficult to let go. They also find it difficult to believe that their legacy may be destroyed, forgotten or reinterpreted. The paradox is thus: the ego and energy that were required to start and maintain a successful business can easily destroy it. The autocratic, overcontrolling, dictatorial, oligarchical alpha male treats his adult mature children like junior reports long after he should have retired to cultivating orchids.

The concept of the family is of course quite wide. A family business may involve blood relations from various generations as well as relations through marriage.

For sociobiologists the issue is all about gene politics. Parents may give equal shares to all their children but this may not be proportional to their desire or ability to run the company. Remember the parable of the prodigal son?

There appears to be various morals that can be learnt from family companies that succeeded and failed over the years. Owner-bosses should understand how and when to retire. This means not hanging on and interfering. It means finding something else to do if the business obsesses them.

Next it means looking for talent outside the family as well as within. This may mean distant relations or more naturally those who are not related to one at all.

Thirdly, expect and allow others to do things differently. The world changes. They may be more in touch with these changes because they are younger. Their (comparative) youth and adaptability may be precisely what the organization needs.

Finally when handing over to the children do so equitably but wisely. This means giving shares and control to those who want it and are good at running businesses. Find something else to leave those who for various reasons don't want to become part of the business.

It is one of those sweet ironies that the more one meddles in family affairs to ensure their longevity the quicker they die.

From private to public

Reports and rumors suggest that successful city types are fleeing the Square Mile to become plumbers, carpenters and artisans of various sorts. They are not "resigning to spend more time with their family" but down-shifting to a happier and less stressful lifestyle.

And there are stories of even former city traders lining up to become managers in the National Health Service. Is this true? Is it another form of downshifting? What could possibly explain it?

Is this a modern myth? Successful, highly paid managers are leaving the private sector preferring to go and work in the public sector?

Cynics have an easy answer: pensions, security, and a relatively unde-manding routine where it is easy to blend in. In fact the pay is not bad and the risks and stress greatly reduced so it seems a very sensible, even a desirable, trade-off for those in the private sector.

But it is probably more complicated than that. First, for someone thinking of leaving a high pressured, but high rewarded, private sector job what else is on offer? Large FTSE 100 companies are certainly high status and high reward. But they are very, very competitive and difficult to break into even with city-based, old-boy, connections. And usually they have no less pressure than the city – so what is the point? No advantage there then.

So smaller companies may look attractive but they usually have lower salary, pay and rations. They may be more family friendly and supportive but they are also more risky. They can more easily go bust or get taken over. And they have lower status (a great concern for the alpha male). Equally importantly there is often no obvious career path or progression. One could easily get trapped.

So the British National Health Service does not look so bad:

- It is known to be good for women at all levels
- It has a family friendly policy and holidays seem generous
- Because it is not driven by the profit motive it seems much more risk-free
- It certainly is a big and famous organization
- One can have significant responsibility for lots of people (at the board level)
- It can be high status: there are good titles (CEO, NED), the possibility of gongs (boys like these) and one may be a local "big wig"

- Pay is competitive given the risk
- And yes, pensions are an issue and will be all the more so

The current climate of the NHS makes it an interesting and important place to work. It has seen massive investment, big numbers PFI and is a major growth area. Indeed many consultancies now float on NHS money. The NHS recognizes that it needs people with experience of dealing with finance in the private sector. And it knows it needs to make jobs attractive to them, so they can seem to be head-hunters for talented but disaffected city types.

Historically the NHS was undermanned and promotion was mainly from within, but now there are lots of trusts and boards that need staffing. Lots of choice and possibilities.

It seems that the NHS will be in the frontline for changing the retirement age, anti-discrimination legislation and so on, all of which can be very attractive to many individuals.

The government has thrown lots of money at the NHS. It is a very hot political issue and likely to remain so. It has lots of shiny new buildings and state-of-the-art computer systems. And so, ironically perhaps, the NHS is *where it is at* in the economy and in politics.

Fundamentalist gurus

Skeptics argue that fundamentalists from all religions appear to have a number of characteristics in common. If you are anti-fundamentalist the traits are dogmatism, obsessionality and intolerance. If you are pro- they articulate clarity, courage and veracity.

Detractors call fundamentalist followers "cults". Supporters see them as "the chosen". Naturally they come in various types depending mainly on their rules and obligations of exclusivity. Most fundamentalists have both orthodox and liberal branches. But those are split again into ultra-orthodox and modernizing liberal.

And they may split often: it is said the Church of God (COG) split into the COG and the True COG; the latter split again into the One True COG and the True COG which split again into the One-and-Only True COG, and so on.

The creed is not revised. The doubters, questioners, alternatives have to form their own coherent, homogenous body of believers.

The essence of fundamentalism is three-fold. First there is clarity about the rules of everything from dress to food. Next there is conservatism and a deep apathy towards change. Thirdly, there is exclusivity (and of course inclusivity) and a demarcation between the "in" and "out" group.

Fundamentalists *know* the truth. There is no room for doubt or skepticism. Relativism and revisionism are revolutionary. There are true believers and the others: heretics, heathens and the damned.

Psychologists talk of uncertainty avoidance and sociologists of intolerance of ambiguity. They interpret a person's attraction to, need for, and acceptance of fundamentalist doctrines as personally important.

The personality, cognitive ability and socialization (education) of individuals in a particular family, society and time lead them to find a happy home among fellow believers.

Some have a need for clarity, certainty and authority. They are attracted to schools, teachers and jobs that give them what they need.

The question is whether there are business fundamentalists. Are there fundamentalist managers? Fundamentalist gurus? Fundamentalist strategists?

Business gurus certainly have things in common with fundamentalist preachers. Watch famous business gurus performing and you see evangelical fervor. You see a man eager to convert believers. You see a man who knows the truth.

But in crucial other ways gurus and some managers are the very opposite of stereotypic fundamentalists. Most encourage, exhort and supposedly welcome change. Away with the old: the past is another country. They are anti-conservative – forever looking for the new.

And they like "thriving on chaos", coping with ambiguity. No obsessional rule following, no right and wrong, black and white. Nothing is or can be clear. And that's OK.

Exclusivity is not an issue either. There are so many mergers and acquisitions that it seems the boundaries are fluid.

But gurus can get evangelically zealous. Their zeal can make them seem fundamentalist, but they may well be cryptic fundamentalists. That is, they have all the characteristics of most fundamentalists but preach the opposite gospel with equal vigor and zealotry.

Some managers have very clear fundamentalist approaches. They can often be found in specialist roles. Try Health and Safety. Here we see a rejoicing in rules and rule enforcement. Things are very clear: you do or do not comply. And if you don't you are a sinner worthy of punishment. You are right or wrong, within or without the rules. And change is not welcome: except of course if it brings more rules.

People with low tolerance to ambiguity seek out schools, hobbies and jobs that do not stress or threaten them. They hate and hence try to avoid uncertainty. They are panicked by existential choice. They like to know the rules and what to do and when.

Creatives of course rejoice in the fudge, the grey and the flexible. Impractical, non-judgemental and possibly hard to pin down.

In religion there is a dimension often described by supporters at the two ends – "fundamentalists" and "liberals". The liberals like to differentiate between the spirit and the letter of the law. The latter enforce the letter. A broad church can embrace both extremes. Business has to. An organization needs both types: it's fundamentally important.

The gullible executive

Every so often a public figure appears to completely go off the rails. They make pronouncements which are odd, weird and wacky. David Icke, the British sports commentator, is, allegedly, the prototype in this field. Normally rational, skeptical and sensible, they adopt absurd conspiracy theories.

But strange ideas are not exclusively the province of individuals. Groups hold conspiracy theories which appear to eschew facts and reason. They hold with passion and conviction some very odd beliefs.

Conversion to wackiness is often the result of stress or misfortune. Stress through having to make too many difficult decisions, too frequently, with little data but profound consequences. Also because it is terrifying to be a victim of seemingly random misfortune, be it illness, accident or deliberate violence. The burden of decision-making and "carrying the can" may cause the sensible executive to suddenly find themselves turning to the wacky world of crystals, numerology or any other pre-enlightenment "jibber-jabber" comforts. Equally, those affected by medically inexplicable or untreatable illness may soon turn, in desperation, to faith and miracle healers who promise the earth (and heaven beyond).

It's not difficult to find examples of pseudo-scientific superstitious believers. It's harder to explain their beliefs and behaviors, particularly in business.

The first obvious answer is that beliefs are psychologically functional. They serve a purpose: to comfort people; to give them a strong sense of identity; to help them make sense of their predicament. Atheists are all in favor of life after death: they just doubt it exists. And they see believers as naive and psycho-logical, not logical. Bad things happen to good people; evil exists and that (alas) is that.

Weird beliefs also provide simple explanations to complex, paradoxical questions. No one wants to live in a world that is utterly mysterious and unpredictable. Or worse – random. We want to live in a *just world*, where good things happen to good people and vice versa. We want explanations for both good and evil. And simple ideas can cut through the Gordian knot albeit totally inappropriately. Indeed the problem of evil is always the hardest issue for the great monotheistic religions.

Science does not do too well at *moral* questions. It seems better at "how" rather than "what" questions. Scientists look for mechanism and process. They try to understand how cancers form and spread, not why some people seem to be targeted. Scientists seem to deal in cold, brutal logic but what people want is *meaning*. They want to make sense of their lives. They want to understand social relations and the future. They yearn for a Disney-like life of warm, kind and benevolent people living in a bountiful world. Wise business people know this. They know they need to give plausible and helpful explanations for success and failure.

Many want these answers to be simple and quick. Immediate gratification is far more attractive than a lifetime's meditation in a Buddhist monastery.

Many executives are talented and hard-working. They try their best in difficult circumstances. They try to be proactive rather than reactive. They try to be good to all their stakeholders. And yet . . . and yet things go wrong. Sometimes out of control. Some people somatize their problem and suffer stress-related illnesses.

But others lose the plot. They can become mentally rigid; have business tunnel vision; even fall into group-think with their "trusted team". The most dangerous reaction is to resort to the pre-, quasi-, anti-scientific world of gurus, mantras and soothsayers who confidently promise magic silver bullets to cure all ills. They sure are tempting. Perhaps that is why so many otherwise reasonable, rational people fall victim to weird wackiness.

Hope springs eternal in every human breast. All people seek for themselves a better life and world. Will intellect and empathy do it? Will reason and compassion suffice? Some doubt it, so they find solace in the unrealistic, unsubstantiated and naive promises of those who propagate half-truths and untruths. And many of these beliefs enshrine both ignorance and intolerance, a dangerous cocktail indeed.

How not to use consultants

Overpaid, overconfident and over here? A simple, but self-important organism designed to translate psychobabble into Swiss bank accounts and air miles? What do we know about management consultants?

At their best they are almost indispensable. They can tumble the numbers in a sophisticated and disinterested way, see trends, benchmark practices and offer excellent advice. They can confront "difficult" managers, confront taboo topics, speak the unspeakable and think the unthinkable. At worst they use your company as a playground for their greed and narcissism. They can demoralize and exacerbate problems.

But why do things sometimes go wrong? Why is their intervention sometimes such an abject failure? Often it is because they have been poorly briefed, poorly managed or expected to do the impossible.

Consultants have to be carefully chosen for their skills, their insights and their fit. They need to be clearly briefed about the desired process and product. This briefing must be explicit and realistic. And there must be flexibility and give so that targets can be adjusted and adapted over time.

When things do go wrong, consultants can leave a situation in a worse state than they found it. Called in to improve the morale or safety consciousness they only worsen it. Asked to reduce shrinkage or absenteeism their efforts effectively increase it.

So ten tips to prevent an unhappy outcome for all concerned:

- Make sure everyone understands why the consultants have (really) been called in. Rumors about their spying or their "real" purpose inhibit them doing their job. They are often seen to be the "Waffen SS" of management, imposing the latter's will on helpless staff.
- Think about the issue of resentment with respect to consultant's daily fees in contrast with those they are counseling, making redundant or instructing. Staff detect massive hypocrisy (albeit misplaced) when they see large amounts of money spent on consultants whose job it is to save costs.
- Make sure the workforce is both briefed and involved. That is, they need to cooperate in any change measure. This means both consultants and managers should get them on board right from the beginning. It is very easy for the whole thing to go wrong through staff resistance. Involvement leads to cooperation.

- Beware the tendency to not search out victims; to blame accidents on staff carelessness; absenteeism on staff neuroticism; strikes on staff political anarchism. Consultants briefed by management should understand that the attribution of blame is often simple-minded, devious and simply wrong. Staff do the same of course, but they blame the management.

- Understand that consultants cannot or should not be used to impose any system, be it appraisal, safety or "comp and ben". They can plan and build systems, but they cannot successfully get them into operation by imposing their power or authority. Consultants can only operate with and through both management and employees to win their support and involvement.

- Consultants need to adapt their language, their techniques and their style to local conditions. This is not to encourage fickle, chameleon-like behavior but the way issues are both presented and solved needs to be done in the language of the organization.

- Consultants love data: on production, rejection, absenteeism. This forms the bread and butter of their analyses. But employees may begin to hide, distort or simply not report data if they believe, in so doing, their job is threatened. Consultants need to be amply aware that taking or recording measures can itself distort the business.

- Management who hire and brief consultants often want the impossible: costs down and revenue up. It is difficult to concentrate on both at the same time. Often there is a trade-off between the two. Expect too much of your consultant; give them "double bind" and they may quite quickly simply pass on the same double-speak message to staff.

- Most problems in organizations are complex and multi-determined. Beware, therefore, the superficial analysis. Consultants have preferred methods from their box of tricks. Some quick and dirty methods yield superficial answers which appear easy to fix but are in truth misleading.

- And beware the under- or over-resourced consultant. The one-man band might seem good value for money but they simply do not have the time to deal with the issues. Likewise the underutilized consultancy might pour people on to the case so that they can, quite simply, keep the order book filled.

Human remains

New psychiatric conditions appear to be discovered on a weekly basis. In the old days, to be a victim of a psychiatric problem was seen as a shameful burden which had to be hidden. And they really were victims: of the system, society, themselves.

Now, however, people appear to be queuing up to receive a diagnosis or a label. It's fashionable to have a condition that explains and excuses. It can mean that you get special, preferential treatment, that you are excused certain tasks or responsibilities.

Further these conditions may well be job linked. Not that people with these problems seek out particular jobs (to which their condition makes them well suited). Rather the stresses and strains lead to having the problem or disorder. A bit like work stress, which is now seen as almost purely a function of a difficult boss, of demanding customers, of long hours, and so on.

What problems might occur in HR; that taxing section (in both senses) of an organization that deals with the soft stuff? Their detractors think R in HR stands for "Remains" because of their attitude and outlook. But we know the soft stuff is hard. People, unlike machines, can be maverick and moody, irritating and irascible, dim and defiant – all of which cause headaches for HR managers.

The following have recently been identified:

1. *Acute change managementism:* The desire to start more and more change management programmes whether or not they are needed and even before the last (failed) one can be properly evaluated.

2. *Adult consultancy dependency:* A regression to a child-like state of dependency on expensive management consultants, who encourage that dependency. This leads to a complete inability to make any decisions without consultants to hand.

3. *Award-seeking addiction:* A total inability not to waste time, money and effort chasing some meaningless government-sponsored industry award, plaque or badge that has no relevance to the real business.

4. *Borderline identity crisis:* This is the constantly gnawing belief that HR is actually unimportant, uninteresting and essentially irrelevant to the business.

5. *Chronic appraisal phobia:* A massive fear of conducting staff appraisals. It can involve rehearsing highly improbable explanations as to why formal appraisals are unnecessary, impossible or unimportant.

6. *Lock-up memory loss:* A fugue-like state that forgets all aspects of HR initiative failure while simultaneously remembering even partial success in detail.

7. *Comp & ben disorder:* An obsessional condition brought on by Hay Point Addiction and legal-cost phobia. It may be accelerated by benchmarking others' salaries.

8. *Creativity finding delusion:* The quite unsubstantiated belief that everyone is creative; that creativity is desirable in everyone; and that a few expensive courses can unblock and unleash creativity even in health and safety experts.

9. *Delayed board-membership ulcer:* A stress condition caused by constant worrying if an HR manager will ever (or worse, deserve to be) promoted to the board.

10. *Email paralysis:* A new condition caused by being so frequently flooded by emails that there is no time to formulate a considered response.

11. *Hysterical high-flyer mania:* This is caused by the belief that particular wunderkinds can be found that will save the business. It involves frantic searches and often ends up by promoting good-looking psychopaths to conditions of power and importance.

12. *Mild meeting madness:* A very common complaint which is the belief that (a) meetings are work, (b) they achieve results, (c) they improve decision-making.

13. *Narcissistic organogram condition:* A delusion caused by obsessive fiddling around with the organization chart in the belief that (a) it is important, (b) anyone pays attention to it, and (c) the profile of HR can be raised by doing so.

14. *Decision procrastination:* A common condition caused by massive discomfort when making tough, explicit decisions about staff cutbacks, lay-offs or pay reductions. It takes many forms and is resistant to cure.

15. *Repetitive innovation syndrome:* This results from both a failure to learn and an addiction to innovation programmes that promise much

and deliver nothing. The result can be innovation phobia on the part of staff.

16. *Repressed psychiatric fantasy condition:* This is the belief that one is a doctor or "ologist" of some repute, trained to help people with their personal problems and conditions.

17. *Restructuring fatigue:* A degenerative disorder that stems from the belief that the solution to all business problems lies in restructuring. The condition is at its worst if people think flattening structures is a simple, problem-free and effective method of increasing profitability.

18. *Teamitus:* The insistence that everyone does and should work in teams. This usually involves commissioning sadistic ex-corporals to teach the benefits (indeed necessity of) interdependent teams on cold and wet Welsh hillsides.

19. *Trainomania:* A classic mania that can easily lead to departmental insolvency. It is spending all one's time and budget either going on every wacky, fashionable and unnecessary course or, worse, coercing others to do likewise.

20. *Shareholder halo illusion:* This is the belief that the shareholders appreciate what one is doing, believe one is important and really care about HR issues. There is a dark-side opposite called "shareholder horns" condition, where shareholders are seen to be evil, money-grabbing and capitalistic.

21. *360-degree disorder:* Like email paralysis, this is a new condition stimulated by consultant magic preaching. It is the belief that if you tell people what others think about them, they will somehow change and improve their performance.

Incommunicado

"Unavailable for comment"; "currently in back-to-back meetings" or "working from home". Read: Too important, too scared or too uninterested to talk to you. The mobile phone and the blackberry have changed the world with respect to communication.

Travel by train or plane or simply walk down the street and you see people of all ages at it everywhere. Just talking . . . business, pleasure, family stuff. They are forever telling others where they are and what they are doing. Unconcerned for either etiquette or ethics, indeed for confidentiality or courtesy; they loudly babble on about daft clients, incompetent bosses and devious colleagues. You hardly need industrial spies any longer. Just catch a train near your target person.

Years ago doctors carried "beepers" both inside and outside hospitals. It was an indication of their importance. But now importance and power and status are not marked by having three mobile phones but by having none.

Mobile-phone users come in various categories. There are the "it's indispensable", "must-have" and "essential for work and leisure" types who obsessively check their phone on a minute-to-minute basis. It becomes a drug. They feel forgotten, ignored, unimportant when not sending or receiving. They sometimes have many phones supposedly for many different purposes. They spend a fortune and make others rich. Some are not far off being "phoneaholics": unable to quit the habit.

Some use their mobile normally – if there is such a thing. Still others admit having them but not using them. They claim never to turn them on. They are there "just for emergencies". Ask when they last used it to find out whether they are telling the truth.

But who would *not* have a phone and why? It is not the poor or the very young or the very old. Eight-year-olds have phones to placate anxious parents; old people welcome them as a sort of emergency panic button. Phone use does not seem to be related to class or caste, rich or poor, urban or rural.

But busy business people have to prioritize communication. They are bombarded by email and snail mail, phone calls and cold calls, even old-fashioned faxes. There are multiple demands on their time all day long.

Ideally you have a filter. Everyone knows the characteristics of the doctor's receptionist. Even blood pouring from three orifices simultaneously is insufficient to pass the barrier.

The communication guard is a filtering system. The task is to establish the purpose of the call and the name, rank and motive of the caller. Fail the filter and you find your target is in a meeting, on a conference call, out of the office.

There are a few tricks one can use. Who is it? Try "The Prime Minister's Policy Unit". "The Today Programme", "Customs and Excise" or "Prince Charles's Private Secretary". That seems to work. It is of course a good trick to find out who is calling *before* indicating whether the person is available or not.

There is one other good reason for being incommunicado. This may appeal more to the paranoid than the snobbish. It is said that with new, high quality, technical equipment you can be literally pin-pointed as to *exactly* where you physically are at any point in time in any place on earth. Your pocket mobile, on or off, enables big brother to watch you from outer space. That should put the wind up a few people claiming to be in one place while being in quite another.

And finally we all know it is more blessed to give than to receive. So cast away your mobile and get a sensible filter system and barrier to anyone trying to contact you.

The incubation period

"Sleep on it" is generally good advice. This is specially true concerning the passion fuelled, impulsive, ill-considered letter of response, first thought of as a good idea.

There is a rich literature on the creative process. Researchers tend to break the area down into four approaches: the creative person; the creative process; the creative product and the creative success. One reason why this remains a bit of a backwater for researchers, however, is because it is often difficult to agree on the creative product. Is the work of Damien Hurst creative success?

Many creative greats have been hailed as creative after that line "They died young, destitute, ignored". Their work unrecognized. Equally, but of course less well-known are those who in their time were heralded as creative geniuses but whose star left the firmament about as quickly as it rose in it.

But we do have enough agreed cases and biographies to begin to understand the process. There are those, for instance, deeply interested in the process of creative writing. How, when and with what did writers write? Did they resist starting until the plot and ending was clear? Did they discipline themselves to write daily or did it all flow out flood-like upon the page?

There seem to be two or three consistent findings in this world. And both contradict those just-buy-my-book, or one-seminar-will-do-it seminars who say that we are all creative. First, people have real talent: ability, genius, flare, call it what you will. They really can write, draw, think. They are well, well above average at their skill. Often the talent is spotted very early – they may have been child prodigies. They have performed at exceptional levels at an exceptional age. Occasionally they just seem superbright being able to read, write, speak multiple languages, and so on incredibly early. But for most, their talent for one particular art form (often music) is richly manifest.

Next there is effort. This means practicing, experimenting, simply getting absorbed by the tools, techniques and technicality of enterprise. Inventors and writers know there are many setbacks and false trails along the highway of success. Henry Ford called it 99% perspiration and 1% inspiration. It can seem remorseless and for the less talented, it probably is. It is in short honing the skills of one's trade.

But creativity is not simply being a good craftsperson or a technically superior worker. It is about doing it differently and better. As we say now it's about thinking "outside the box". Turning the idea on its head. Doing it differently. Combining things never combined before. Thinking the impossible and doing it.

And this is where the incubation period comes in. Many people say they have their best ideas on the beach while on holiday, driving on a long trip, even in the bath at the weekend.

Solutions come seemingly spontaneously not specifically when they are being sought. But they do not come magically. The groundwork has to have been done. The problems need already to have been examined in considerable detail for a reasonable period of time – by the talented person.

Are these sparks of genius the result of the workings of the (murky) unconscious? Have they been expressed by powerful and mysterious intra-psychic forces? Probably not. People do report that solutions, inspirations and visions have come to them in dreams but that is pretty rare.

A better metaphor might be a cloud-swept sky where clouds quickly and spontaneously change their shape and spatial arrangement one with another. Suddenly the impossible jigsaw suggests a solution.

So sleep on it. But don't hope for much unless you have worked at the problem first. Oh dear, just as always, success is determined by effort and ability. Not luck. And no funny colored hats. Just ability with effort and a nice touch of incubation.

Inoculating the workforce

Trainers talk rather disparagingly of "sheep dipping" an organization or a department. Amused by their herding theme they often talk of "corralling" the delegates and "putting them through" a programme.

What they usually mean is that everybody in a department, or perhaps the whole organization, is *mandated* to go on a course. The reasons may be many. It could be a legal requirement, emanating out of a Brussels diktat or from Westminster, or some trade legislation. It may be simply that the CEO likes it. It may be a job-creation scheme designed by the trainers themselves.

All courses have multiple aims and multiple outcomes. These can frequently be summarized as knowledge, skills and understanding. That is, the attendees are supposed to gain new useful and practical knowledge at the end of the course that they did not have at the beginning.

Delegates are also told they will have a deeper, richer, salient understanding of people, processes or products. They will (or should) be able to comprehend company policy, competitive strategy and customer demands. Understanding is itself knowledge.

And, of course most courses claim that they are primarily in the business of skills teaching. These may be new skills, or advanced skills or top-up skills. People should come away after three days outside their office to do something that is both relevant to their job and of course value to themselves.

A second consequence of any course, be it planned or serendipitous, is that people get to know each other better. Separated in their so-called "silos", people at the same level from marketing and manufacturing, planning and production, accounts and advertising meet each other in nice hotels and training rooms.

Propinquity is the best predictor of friendship at work. And perhaps minimal or nil contact the best predictor of uncooperativeness. Some organizations understand this well and see courses as much for bonding as learning events.

But there is another function of courses, indeed all big company events. And it is psychological, possibly propagandist. It's about ideology, the faith, the party line. Often people in sales do this the best, because they know its value and power.

Salespeople face everyday continuous rejection: Politely and impolitely, explicitly and implicitly, coyly and assertively, people say "No". They do not like, want or rate the product. Salespeople have to keep going. They need to be resilient, determined, hardy. They need to approach each new, potential customer with a fresh, enthusiastic and concentrated start.

It's too easy to blame the product, the organization, the customer, or worse, oneself for lack of success. That way leads to disaster. It probably accounts for remarkable attrition rates in salespeople which can be as high as 95% over a year. Worse, they are often on their own being the lonely long-distance salesperson.

So they need to get together to celebrate success: to rehearse the party line: to sell the product to themselves. They need promotional rejuvenation.

Conferences can be about renewing the faith. Politicians know this at their annual bash. But workers need to hear more than why they, the product and their management are the best. They need to know what is wrong with the competition.

In many divinity degrees, particularly if taught by Jesuits, there is a course on apologetics. This is not about apologizing for being a believer. Rather, it is a defense or vindication of the belief system. Its tactic is to take all the objections – Freudian, Humanist, Marxist – and show where they are flawed. The idea is not to surprise or confound the believer but provide him (and it still is always "him" as a Jesuit) with ammunition.

Most workforces also need inoculating against the slings and arrows of outrageous fortune. They need to know how to respond to criticism, complaint and objection. They need antiviral, ideological inoculation. That is, they need to expect but be able to deal with doubters inside and outside the organization.

The troops need to be rallied, to be encouraged but also to be inoculated. Good managers know this and they know how to do it. Indeed it can be very inspiring. And with the right mix of soundbite, humor and insight a whole course and workforce can face the world more hardily, more stoically and even more productively.

Integrity tests

What is the single most important characteristic people want in their boss? Supportiveness, emotional intelligence, vision? No. Straightforwardness, courage, ambition. No again. The answer is integrity.

In a world of spin and branding, of buying and selling, the concept of integrity seems forgotten. Even the word has the ring of another era. But integrity has come back to bite those who ignored it. Both front and business pages of newspapers and magazines are crowded with stories of the great and the good who lied, stole and cheated their way to fame and destruction.

The problem has become so serious in some circles that managers are considering "testing" for integrity at selection. We all know about ability tests and personality tests, but what about integrity tests? But they are now big business. Their mounting popularity has been put down to an increase in theft and fraud, drug and alcohol problems, cases of bullying and violence, and so on.

There are options open to those who are interested in, or stress the necessity of honesty screening. They could buy or hire a polygraph or lie detector. Some organizations spend a lot of money on vetting candidates' background and credentials. Others try urine or blood testing. Some try careful biographical application form testing.

Most believe they conduct some sort of integrity interviewing, but many are turning to standardized questionnaires.

"Preposterous" is the cry of those always intractably opposed to any form of self-report. People lie on these things and liars lie the most. Thus paradoxically the "innocent" hard-working individuals who may (honestly) admit to a few trivial and essentially irrelevant indiscretions are labeled "dishonest", while psychopathic delinquents lie through their teeth and come out smelling only of roses.

This is for many the Achilles heel of tests: the problem of misclassification, particularly the innocent being judged guilty, the honest dishonest and those with integrity assumed to lack it.

Some people argue that dishonesty is both culturally determined and highly variable. Dishonesty and lack of integrity are not characteristics of individuals, but a response to very specific situational factors.

So do integrity tests work? Is there evidence that these relatively simple questionnaires can detect whether people are more or less likely to engage in dishonest, counterproductive behaviors? Can they predict who will be honest or dishonest? There are various ways of checking the reliability of tests. They include:

1. The "known" or contrast groups method. People who are known to be both honest and dishonest are given the test and the quantity and quality of the difference in response is recorded.
2. Background, biographical check. A thorough background check using police, school, and organizations' records is related to test scores.
3. Admissions and confessions. Separate (perhaps confidential) admissions to a wide range of dishonest behaviors from the trivial to the very serious, are correlated with test scores.
4. Predictive or future method. People are tested at organizational entry and scores are related to documented (proven) dishonest behaviors over their careers.
5. Time-series or historic method. Before honesty tests are used in selection, all sorts of indices are collected e.g. loss, shrinkage. The same data are collected after tests are used in selection to see if there is a noticeable difference.
6. Correlations with polygraph or anonymous admissions of theft or absenteeism.

Certainly tests have been validated against very different criteria, for example theft, faking credentials, "counter-productive" behavior and they do tend to produce rather different results. Working on company time, taking long lunch breaks are called "time theft". Stealing office stationary (pens, paper) is strictly theft. But both of these could be considered trivial, certainly quite different from the theft of company secrets, or of valuable products used for production or the products themselves.

But what is the latest thinking around these tests? First, it is agreed that they are useful. They predict dishonesty. They are valid enough to help prevent various problems. Secondly, testing alone won't stop all theft, dishonesty, or sabotage as many factors other than dishonest individuals can cause them. A systems approach is needed. Thirdly, integrity tests may be measuring aspects of human personality which are stable over time. Research suggests that integrity is related to morality, a stable trait.

Fourthly, there are problems in testing because some testing codes and standards insist that testees give informed consent on details about the test such as what it measures. Hardly the best thing to give the dishonest person! Fifthly, there may be legal issues in how "cut-off" scores are used and labeled. One could classify people as pass/fail or very, highly, moderately dangerous. How this information is used or recorded can cause expensive legal action. So is the game worth the candle? Sixthly, integrity tests are used to "select out", not "select in". They are designed to help people screen out high-risk applicants, not identify "angels".

A major issue for all organizations, however, is how people react to the idea of being tested for their integrity. It seems they react to the concept of integrity-testing roughly similarly, irrespective of the type of test used. One American study found the following:

- 90% felt it was appropriate for an employer to administer such a test.
- 4% would refuse to take such a test.
- 63% would enjoy being asked to take such a test.
- 11% felt this type of test was an invasion of privacy.
- 2% said if they had two comparable job offers, they would reject the company using such a test.
- 3% would resent being asked to take such a test.
- 82% felt that a test such as this is sometimes an appropriate selection procedure.
- 5% believe that administering a test such as this reflects negatively on the organization.
- 80% indicated that being asked to take such a test would not affect their view of the organization.
- 80% indicated that tests such as this are routinely used in industry.

So. A cost-effective, increasingly important screening necessity? Or a dangerous improbable gimmick? As likely to lead to legal costs as identifying villains?

It all depends. But there seems to be one reasonable and sensible conclusion. Used judiciously and in conjunction with other measures that also provide valid data, these tests can certainly alert one to the possibility that given due cause to be dishonest, some individuals would much more happily do so than others.

Job fit in plain speak

Vocation guidance is a pretty simple concept about helping round pegs into round holes and square pegs into square holes. Yes, people and jobs are complex. Yes, they change – well jobs do at any rate.

And yes, some jobs are quite simply much more attractive than others. But it is patently obvious that people are happier, healthier and more productive when they are in certain roles in certain types of organization than in other types of employment. The question is how, when and where to give them vocational guidance?

Job fit involves a parsimonious description of an individual's preferences/predilections and abilities. It also involves, preferably using the same language, description of jobs, tasks, roles and responsibilities. Then the match, or fit, between the person and the job becomes (more) apparent.

Let's start with personality. Research for over a century trying to find the periodic table of personality has led in the past twenty years to broad agreement among researchers in the area. There are five independent, probably biologically based and partly genetically determined traits. These traits are inherent (deeply rooted), consistent in their behavioral manifestations and relatively immutable (fixed) and difficult to change. For an adult what you see is what you've got.

Thus some people are talkative, sociable, self-confident. They like other people and tend to be socio-centers. They are comfortable in groups and teams and enjoy intensive and extensive people (that is, customer, peer, subordinate) contact. Other are quiet, retiring, apparently shy. They prefer to work alone and have a much lower need for social contact of all kinds. This, of course, is *introversion–extroversion.*

The salient question here is about social contact at work: with colleagues and total strangers (that is, customers). People can be excited, enlivened and energized by social contact, or frightened and exhausted by the same prospect. Long-distance lorry drivers, authors, gardeners tend to be introverts. Salespeople, cabin crew, hotel receptionists tend to be extroverts. But people still get it wrong. They often think introverts are happy as librarians. They tend to make unhappy librarians because the job involves extensive (and growing) customer contact.

Next, some people tend to be sunny, cheerful, warm and empathic while others are dour, unsympathetic, grumpy. This is about being hard or soft-hearted. It's about sensitivity to and interest in the feelings of others.

Tender vs tough-minded. Trusting vs cynical. Friendly vs unfriendly. This dimension is called *agreeableness*. It certainly relates to customer-service skills. Nurses, social workers and primary-school teachers, indeed all those dealing with the vulnerable, need to be agreeable. It must come naturally. And it can be a handicap when agreeable managers have to deal with recalcitrant, incompetent and disagreeable staff. Their natural warmth and kindness may prevent them from "kickin' ass" as hard and frequently as they should.

Thirdly, some people are curious, imaginative and artistic, while others are conventional, practical and focused. This dimension is called *openness to experience*, as it is related to creativity, a life of the mind, to possibilities rather than practicalities. The more open people are the more prone to boredom. They think outside the box too much. You do not want creative airline pilots whose job it is to sit in small, dark, cool spaces watching computers for hours. Neither do you want openness in those dealing with rule-enforcement in security and safety. But you want it in shovelfuls when working in Research and Development, Marketing and Design.

But the last two characteristics are the most important. And they both apply to nearly all jobs. Some people are calm, contented and placid. They are stable under fire, resilient and emotionally robust. Others are easily upset, tense, anxious, moody and highly strung. This is what your grandparents called "having nerves", you called it *neuroticism* and your children are having to call it "negative affectivity". It is, in short, the ability to handle pressure and stress.

Most jobs have some sources of stress – tight deadlines, disgruntled customers, competing demands, indolent staff, tough performance standards. One rule of thumb is that the higher you go, the greater your responsibilities (and commensurate reward) and hence more pressure. The unstable soon cave in with psychosomatic illness (ulcers, irritable bowel, migraines), depression or erratic behavior. They are a menace to themselves, their colleagues and the business.

Stress is inevitable. The question is how well-resourced people are to cope with it. Being a police officer, or a taxi driver, or a journalist or a dentist or a CEO means daily stress. Some cope better than others. Be sure to get this one right. It's a serious and major cause of job misplacement.

And finally, there is *conscientiousness*, the work ethic, diligence, prudence or whatever. Some people are (and probably always have been) hardworking, self-disciplined and well organized. Others are (alas) disorganized, easily distracted and undependable. Most employers want an efficient, reliable and thorough employee. And they eschew (read reject) the frivolous, hedonistic, egocentric.

This is more than simply being ambitious. It's more about achievement orientation and drive for results. Conscientious people have self-discipline, self-starting drive and a sense of direction. If the job requires dedication, long hours and 100% input (for just rewards), this is the characteristic you want. Conscientious people stay on and come in when required over and above what it says in their contract. They have drive and are driven. They just need a direction and an appropriate reward.

So what sort of people make good home-based remote workers or long-distance truck drivers or proofreaders or call-center staff? Who would thrive as a stage director or an aromatherapist or a chef? The trick is not to be dazzled by the television images of these jobs or of particular individuals who hardly represent the occupation in the first place. It's just as simple or complex as it has always been. Do a job analysis: understand what and how people are required to do things and then search for those best fitted to the job.

Living in Sweden

Is it perhaps the gravadlax? Or the long dark winters? The price of claret? Could be a curious combination of the above?

But Sweden is apparently a sick society. Not sick morally or socio-emotionally. Not even sick financially any more, but physically sick.

The evidence. According to the Swedish Confederation of Enterprises three statistics are overwhelming. *One in ten* of the workforce call in sick *every day*. *Over half a million* (of nine million total) have retired early on sickness pensions. And in the dark north the average worker takes on average *70 days off per annum*.

This is serious stuff and has massive effects on the Swedish economy. For the simple-minded there are essentially two explanations. The first is that for some reason work is very stressful in Sweden, or at least the work–life balance is or the climate is. That is, the statistics speak to a miserable, hard life: short, nasty and brutish.

But in Sweden? Surely not. Remember how the lefties in the 1970s and 80s dismissed Russian socialism as distorted but Swedish socialism as pure: *The* model. Generous state provisions for everything. Heavy comprehensive legislation to prevent exploitative employers. Powerful trade unions. And high living standards. Having your cake and eating it? So it seemed.

The cynics never believed the hype. They took satisfaction in the end of Swedish hubris when a decade ago Swedish public deficit exceeded 10% of GDP. The moral, the experiment, the mirage was over.

Practical, pragmatic realists they began to change never-never-land. Politicians spoke more honestly and less optimistically. Education had priority over benefits. Central government took more control over local authorities. And things improved.

But they haven't conquered the "sickness thing". And there are real lessons for all of us. It is not about compassion but about differentiation. It is about those old Victorian versions of knowing and understanding the difference between the *deserving* and the *undeserving* poor and sick.

Swedes are rightly regarded as clever, adaptable and dedicated. They are loyal and dependable. But they have forgotten some of the central tenets of the work ethic. The problem is it has become normative to be stressed and sick. Normative means acceptable, commonplace, average. Swedes still think if you feel tired, your nursery school is on strike or you feel there is a lot of work conflict, it is perfectly acceptable to take time off.

People see their friends and neighbors gardening happily on sick leave. They see others, apparently fit and rigorous retired at 60 even 55. Social comparison is invidious. Swedes don't accept the idea that large numbers are cheating the system, faking illness, or, worse, fraudulently claiming sick benefits while working. But they do accept the fact that the sickness culture has to change.

But corporate or national change is difficult. It takes time. One has to be very persistent and very determined. It means using carrots and sticks in both the public and private sector. Just as we receive a no-claims bonus with insurance companies, so people could be rewarded with extra pay or time for a good attendance records.

Suggest that we need to reduce the sickness-normative culture and the cries of "unfair", "exploitative" even "illegal" are soon heard.

Everyone accepts the point that people do get sick. They also have sick relatives. Frankly, little at work is important if your child is sick. We also accept that people get stressed at work. And it is patently obvious that some are more prone to stress than others.

But this is not to encourage the sick role. Most people's reaction to seeing others take "time off" they think is not strictly illness-related is to do likewise. That is equitable. Why should I carry a colleague? Why should they have time off and not me? So I too will claim illness.

And that is where the vicious cycle begins. The slide into an absenteeism, sick-time-off culture. Reversing the cycle is not easy as the Swedes have found.

You do not have to punish the really sick in reversing the sick-role culture.

Managing the post-materialist employee

Do you believe in science, technical progress and the benefits of economic growth? Do you approve of democracy and the big institutions in our society such as governments, schools, churches and trade unions? Do you respect the law and those trying to uphold and enforce it? Do you believe that everyone has family and social obligations?

You do? Oh, dear! How old-fashioned! How modernist! Has no one told you about post-modernism and it's sister post-materialism?

There are many interesting academic questions to ask about post-materialism. There are *historical* questions about the origins of both materialism and post-materialism. There are *anthropological* questions about the impact of culture on post-materialism and, more interestingly perhaps, vice versa. There are *sociological* questions about the distribution of post-materialist values in society. There are *psychological* questions about how post-material beliefs affect behavior and how easy it is to change these beliefs.

But there are also *managerial* questions about how to manage the post-material employee. How to motivate them? Whether to attempt to select or deselect them? How to match them to their customers?

Perhaps the materialist/post-materialist classification is too simple? Perhaps there are crypto, neo, quasi materialists, all rather mixed up about what they believe and value. Equally there may be confused post-materialists who rather yearn for the lifestyle of materialists.

Best start with those we know best. *Materialist Man* can be unfairly and crudely stereotyped. Greed is good. He who has most toys wins. Survival of the richest.

Materialist man is homo-economicus. A relatively simple organism designed to increase his or her happiness by wealth accumulation, which is believed to be good for all. Materialist man is logical, rational, objective at work. Readily incentivized by money, status, security and the like. Work is the price you pay for money. Money brings, freedom, choice, love, power, security and respect. To have is to be.

Most of the more serious management books are designed to help people manage materialist man. They are prototypically white collar, social class IIIa or above, reasonably educated. They have invested a lot in their society, as it is, and happy (and very eager) to reap the rewards of that society. Managers and employees know where they stand.

Crypto Materialist Man is often a child of the sixties and has been exposed to the beliefs and values of post-materialism through various groups. This may be expressed through mysticism, self-exploration or, indeed more likely, ecological awareness.

Crypto materialist man is a hopeful downshifter, believing that you have to be rich enough to afford post-modern values. So you play the game, support the system, make your pile and then act out "the Good Life". Along the way, you do a lot of recycling, support wind farms (a long way from where you live) and buy "fair trade" goods.

Crypto materialists come in different packages. They may be people in a hurry to escape. They know the rules and are probably very easy to manage. They may seem egocentric and hypocritical, but read them right and they are not difficult to supervise. Some, however, are failed materialists who find comfort in the post-materialist message. It can be a good way of sniping at, as well as attacking, those they envy.

Crypto Post-Materialist Man are those who chant the mantra well but enjoy *Hello* magazine and all that it stands for. They can't quite let go of the baubles of materialism. They can be haunted by the idea that life is short: it is not a dress rehearsal. They also know the earth is filled with good things which they would like to experience. Fly first-class to Hawaii. Own a Roller. Have a pile in France.

Crypto post-materialists vacillate. They are therefore difficult to predict. Old hippies, young people, the dispossessed: all may find a spiritual home in the post-materialist message but secretly yearn for the benefits of materialism. They need to be very subtly managed. What you see is not what you get. A manager needs to be imaginative (that is, sly, devious perhaps) in how to direct, reward and motivate them.

Post-Material Man either may not or cannot be managed, because they don't work for big for-profit organizations. They are into self-expression, creativity and harmony. They work out their own value system and have little time for all those triumphs of the enlightenment, such as democracy and the big institutions of law, education and business.

Post-materialist man always emphasizes quality over quantity; being, over having; subjectivity, over objectivity. They may happily "work" together in communes, collectives and consortia but can be surprisingly dictatorial about non-dictatorial behavior.

It is easy to be cynical about strong advocates of both materialism and post-materialism. Certain time periods – the sixties, the eighties – seem to epitomize the heyday of their belief systems. And people, usually young people at a critical period of their development of their ideological and value systems, may be perpetually marked (indeed scarred) by a belief system. Thus they are at some level carriers of the flame which has to be hidden when the zeitgeist is against them – hence the cryptos and the generation-gap stuff.

Old hippies and generation X may therefore have a lot in common, as may children of the 50s and 80s. Values are not discussed much at work – except through the anodyne platitudes of mission and vision statements. Yet a person's values will have a direct impact on the management style which will bring out the best in them.

Management psychiatry

Compared to many other professionals, psychiatrists appear to have been uncharacteristically coy and reticent to offer their services and expertise to the business world. Whilst many have met prominent business people (patients) who have succumbed to the many temptations and stresses of corporate life, psychiatrists have tended to be *reactive* rather than *proactive* in passing on their insights.

There are some psychiatrists interested in how and why individuals with a mix of problems fail and derail. They have been particularly good at identifying, describing and categorizing syndromes in the dark side of behavior at work.

Critics of psychiatry say that it will remain on the starting blocks until researchers stop squabbling about the names and contents of their various diseases, problems and syndromes and start to explain their causes. And, of course, provide effective cures.

And skeptics often wonder how serious this medical speciality is when every month or so they seem to discover a new syndrome which either excuses or explains away some selfish, antisocial behavior. There certainly seems to be a long queue of individuals happy to eschew personal and moral responsibilities for their behavior by being diagnosed with some (terrible) affliction which is not their fault.

Further, there is some doubt as to whether long established mental illness terms like "neuroticism" and "psychoticism" are actually useful. Some think they are too inclusive, often masking real differences between subgroups of illnesses. Some people believe that all they do is serve to label and thus make the problem worse. Patient groups have fought orthodox psychiatrists and made them back down about the use of labels.

But, enter business psychiatry. Surely there is a ripe niche for psychiatric language and labels to capture the frankly odd and bizarre behavior that so many experience at work. Perhaps the following may make a useful beginning:

1. *Residual administrative fetish:* The inability of someone well trained in administrative bureaucracy to "let go" the four-forms-to-do-anything approach. At the highest level it means limited delegation, defaulting on "no" and being over-fascinated by procedure.

2. *Borderline budgetary mania:* This may be linked to both the lunar and the solar cycles and lead to light-headed, lunatic behavior. It occurs at

the time any sort of budget must be submitted. The mania can be bipolar in bear and bull markets.

3. *Periodic committee obsession:* This is the delusional belief that committees improve the quality of decisions rather than just take the blame. It involves forming committees and subcommittees that take minutes but waste hours, giving the illusion of doing work and with little positive outcome.

4. *Post-traumatic customer service reaction:* A serious chronic condition suffered by those on helplines, complaint desks and customer service departments through experiencing endless angry, frustrated and demanding clients.

5. *Adolescent delegation behavior:* The uncontrollable need to delegate responsibility and more often blame when anything goes wrong. This is an affective disorder because it is accompanied by strong outbursts of varied emotions, insults and sulking withdrawal.

6. *Intermittent efficiency fixation:* The nature of this rare condition is that is appears to occur without any specific cause but has drastic consequences. Sufferers very suddenly decide everything has to change and everything is too expensive. Thus, mad, highly fashionable, management ideas are suddenly and warmly embraced to improve efficiency, and equally quickly dropped.

7. *Dysfunctional entrepreneurial deficit:* The plight of newly privatized companies who try but fail in the marketplace. Quite unused to customer service, market discipline or performance management, an individual tries and fails to emulate popular entrepreneurs at all levels.

8. *Atypical ethical fetish:* A late onset complaint often associated with private-life changes, that sees all behavior at work as having an ethical dimension. Like Tourette's Syndrome, it is characterized by inappropriate vocalization of irrelevant issues during meetings to gain attention.

9. *Episodic greed tendency:* Found mostly in city firms, this is a group-based illness akin to a feeding frenzy of piranhas or vultures. It is the sudden loss of reason or perspective at annual bonus time and involves the almost total loss of altruism and perspective.

10. *Habitual health and safety neurosis:* An obsessive illness possibly unresponsive even to Cognitive Behavior Therapy. It involves mainly

preventing things from occurring and the installation of fences, doors, washbasins and odd, pointless rituals.

11. *Bipolar industrial relations psychosis:* This is the New Labour disease where managers are not sure whose side they are on – shareholders or employees. They happily hold, in their belief systems, contradictory ideas which they can even articulate together at an Islington dinner party. At worst involves the inability to distinguish between HR, IR or PR.

12. *Habitual inflationary malady:* This occurs not only in marketing departments but also in organization's service departments, particularly in good years.

13. *Chronic innovation impulse:* An irrational desire constantly to find and deploy so-called creative people and ideas to all aspects of the business. Innovation is thought to be essential and introduced so frequently that before any idea, process or concept is fully understood or implemented, it is discarded.

14. *Abnormal loyalty withdrawal:* This is the sudden onset of POPO (Passed Over and Pissed Off) behavior. It occurs after mergers and acquisitions or promotion announcements. It involves a middle-aged executive's sudden total disengagement and a "quit but stay" attitude. Phrases like "Not in my job description", "We tried that but failed" regularly occur.

15. *Delusional marketing malady:* The belief that marketing is at the heart of the business. It is an egocentric point of view held by people who only mix with their own department and has, therefore, cult-like qualities. Delusions include the belief that consumer behavior is at the same time determined by unconscious forces and is predictable.

16. *Unconscious power fixation:* This occurs at any age and it is the irrational belief that certain job titles bring deserved and magic power. It concerns fantasises that people will obey your every command and fulfill every wish. It completely decouples power from responsibilities.

17. *Acute profit-taking reaction:* This is a corporate hands-in-the-till disorder which occurs only at certain periods of time, usually associated with change. This can be precipitated by regulatory change or impending takeover.

18. *Intermittent quality control dysfunction:* What is oddest about this problem is that it seems unprovoked, or precipitated by very minor issues.

Individuals, often little bothered by process, suddenly become overwhelmingly concerned with semi-trivia in various parts of the quality-control process.

19. *Substance-induced secretarial compulsion:* This is a Christmas-party and summer-outing malady which renders people apparently different under non-work conditions. It may take various forms such as finding someone who one works with on a day-to-day basis overwhelmingly physically attractive or repulsive and having to let them know it.

20. *Adolescent teamwork impulse:* This is a mood-based disorder involving teamwork. It may mean individuals do daft things together in the name of working better. It is a set of pointless, expensive and distracting activities that lead to work avoidance.

21. *Undifferentiated technology obsession:* A complaint often associated with adolescent boys, involving a desire to have the latest gadgets all over the organization. Some sufferers are addicts of science fiction and find it difficult to understand current reality. This is correlated with a high-obsolescence budget. Sufferers have the delusion that "future-proofing" technology is more than a sales gimmick.

Money as a motivator

The single most frequently asked question of management consultants is about how better to motivate staff. Every manager wants a happy, healthy, but highly productive staff. Ideally they are intrinsically motivated by the sheer joy of the job: but if not, one has to think about extrinsic rewards.

And the most obvious of all extrinsic rewards is money. And so we have the very simple-minded view that "if you pay people peanuts you will get monkeys". That is, that there is a simple relationship between reward, productivity and satisfaction. The idea is that better paid people are more productive and happy. Simple, causal, naive and essentially evidence-free.

Indeed there are at least four reasons why money is seen by business psychologists as much more likely to be a cause of dissatisfaction than satisfaction.

The first reason relates to the simple idea that there is a clear correspondence between pay and performance. This is not, nor has ever been, true. Perceived low pay can and does lead to considerable dissatisfaction and demotivation but not vice versa.

The effects of a pay rise very soon wear off as people adapt to their new conditions. Any improvements are therefore likely to be very temporary. Money can be a very effective motivator but you need a great deal of it to stop adaptation effects. Too much for most organizations to bear.

Secondly, what leads to pay satisfaction is not so much absolute salary but comparative salary. So if my salary goes up dramatically, but so does that of my comparison group, there is no change in my behavior. This is crucial and relates to the whole problem of performance-related pay as we shall see. No matter what people are paid, if they believe, with or without evidence, that they are not *equitably and fairly* paid they become demotivated.

Thirdly, *money is not everything*. Many would be happy with more time off or more job security than more money. People are prepared to trade-off things for money once they have enough or grow weary of the game which is not worth the candle.

Finally, there is the eternal implication of tax and spend: all very well to increase pay but if increased taxes eat heavily into it where is the benefit? Why earn when the government take too much?

Many people in the public sector see salary increases merely as government attempts to "catch up" with the times: to align pay and conditions with the private sector. It was, and is, an attempt at the restitution of justice.

That is, they do not see the connection between input (namely productivity) and output (money).

They come from a sector that for a very long time had a service-related management system. That is, loyalty and service, not customer satisfaction or measurable productivity, were rewarded. But now we have performance-related management systems (PMS) which cause manifest problems.

The PMS system seems logical and fair. It is essentially the way we pay sales people: low base-rate, high commission. There is a clear logical and equitable relationship between personal effort and outcome and reward. It is essentially a piece-rate system. It works well. But we do know that the attrition rate in sales staff is incredibly high (over 90% in the insurance industry) and that the distribution of salaries is incredibly skewed.

We know, and have done for a hundred years, that the productivity of the most productive worker is always two to three times that of the least productive worker. So we should reward them appropriately and equitably. Not equally and not based on service/experience or loyalty.

Fine, if you can measure productivity easily and well. For most senior and sophisticated jobs it is difficult to get objective, sensible, comparative measures of output. How do you measure the output of a police officer, or a bank manager or a professor? Of course you can find measures. Professors are assessed by the number of books and papers that they write; how often they are cited; the amount of money they attract for the university and of course student evaluations. But still they are not paid equitably. It would simply cause far too much discontent.

Indeed this is why so often institutions keep all salaries secret. The reason is that it reduces social comparison. But whatever one does, people get angered and frustrated by perceived inequity. It seems the clearer one makes the relationship, the more upset people get, particularly those in power who have lived under the old regime and they had "earnt" their right to power, influence and money. Hence the dissatisfaction with these systems and organizations abandoning them.

Another big error is to assume a simple, linear and causal relationship between salary and efficiency that goes something like this: make people happy at work with nice offices, free meals, competitive salaries, and they experience work satisfaction. This in turn leads to greater performance and efficiency.

But there is very little good evidence that satisfaction leads to productivity. It is the same mistake made about self-esteem, where it is assumed that esteem leads to achievement, happiness and success rather than the other way round.

It may be much wiser to invest in better productivity than satisfaction, because the causal path is more that way round. Thus the productive worker is better rewarded, more positively appraised and gains more confidence.

The public sector still reflects the *service* rather than the *performance* ethic. Loyalty, years of service, a clean sheet, good reputation, determine promotion much more than performance measured by output, customer feedback and so on.

If you want efficiency you have to measure it, understand the process, set goals/targets and reward their achievement. You need to understand how teams work together in doing so. It is easy to set goals but harder to measure and understand how they are achieved. If there is no clear relationship between effort and reward by individuals and their team, there seems little incentive to be more productive.

An entrepreneur would soon stop pouring money down the drain if he or she thought that spending was not leading to efficiency. They would first start looking at delivery systems and structures to see if they were working properly. If not, there would be a strong dose of *process re-engineering*. Yes, that fad is a bit passé now, but the idea is fundamental. Is efficiency a function of a poorly designed system that can be improved? If yes, redesign, even if there is a lot of resistance.

If the systems and structure are OK select and train people to work it well. This may mean losing those unable or unwilling to adopt new ways of working. The motto is *"be happy here or be happy elsewhere"*. Then make sure you have a way to identify and reward productivity and efficiency equitably.

No quick fix, alas: hard words for politicians to hear. But otherwise so little effect for so much tax payers' money. And when they understand that, it seems quite reasonable to turn to others who may have some better ideas, a longer view and more courage to make changes that really work.

Nepotism, corruption and incompetence

Consider the following three agony-aunt problems, and whether you agree with the response:

> My boss got his first wife a job in the organisation. He did likewise with his second wife who has neither talent nor any sign of the work ethic. Now he is putting pressure on me to "select" his under-qualified son for a job in my department. What should I do?

Nepotism and patronage in general are extremely common. A glance at the BBC reveals numerous examples of the children of the famous having had jobs (Dimbleby, Magnusson, and so on). Some argue that it is evidence of genuine talent being passed on from one generation to the next. Others see children modeling their parents and learning early about the skills and lifestyle associated with the job. Cynics see it as pure corrupt nepotism.

Nepotism is considered normal, indeed desirable in many cultures. Keeping jobs within the family can be economically prudent and ensure that control is kept within the confines of the "clan". Further, a manager of a relation has a great deal of useful data about their ability, personality, work style and motivation.

However, the downside of in-family favoritism is the employment of someone who is clearly not suited to the job, or at least there may be others who are much more suitable. The relative may not be bright enough – a sausage short of a fry-up; too neurotic to deal with demanding customers; too laid-back to do much work. Once they are in place they experience the patronage of their powerful, protective parent. And everyone suffers – the manager of the nepotised nonentity, his or her peers, subordinates, customers, and eventually the organization as a whole.

It is not easy to stand up to one's boss over this one. One trick is to get an outside, disinterested, consultant to conduct an impartial, if expensive, appraisal. Another is to approach your boss's boss, confidently asking his or her opinion. A third is to have organizational rules about the selection of relatives (by both blood and marriage). Your boss needs to hear a clear message now, otherwise the problem will escalate and continue:

> Over the past years a good supplier of ours has invited me to various parties. We have spent a good deal of money with this firm but not much in the past

18 months. In the last two days I have received a very generous "gift" from the "local rep" worth many hundreds of pounds. Should I accept it?

When is a gift a bribe? Many salespeople abuse our sense of reciprocity. Hence the success of wine-tasting sessions. One may only consume about 50p worth of wine, but then feel obliged to buy a case of mediocre, over-priced plonk precisely to "pay back" the salesperson's generosity.

Members of many organizations no doubt now deeply regret accepting a range of gifts from business people. Be it a night in an expensive Parisian hotel, a fact-finding-mission, first-class air fare or a nice car. The "gift" does not come free. Just as there is no such thing as a free lunch, so there is often no such thing as a "free gift".

But gift-giving is an important part of culture and it would be sad to attempt to stop the process. The author of a book is proud to give away a copy; the artist, likewise, a picture. Many companies try to solve the problem by imposing a maximum value on gifts which may be accepted. This may be anything as low as £10.00, above which the gift has to be reported and logged.

The central question must be the motive. Some gifts are really little more than advertisements and harmless as such. Some are quite frankly an attempt to get rid of old stock. But some are quite obviously meant as an "inducement", which may be a kinder word than bribe.

Questions to ask yourself are these: Who is the present for? Is it for your personal use or for the office as well? Are you expected to keep it private or do you think the giver wants others to know about it? Is it a product made by the company and a sort of advertisement?

If you are made uncomfortable by the whole thing, simply drop the giver a short note saying that, alas, company policy prevents you from receiving personal presents and although you very much appreciate the thought you simply cannot accept the "gift". No offense meant:

> We have recently started a performance management system which requires my boss to fill out a long questionnaire on my performance over the year. He is supposed to have had a meeting with me in the summer to discuss it. However, he simply evades all attempts to talk about it and refuses to show me the completed forms.

Incompetent managers are frequently pusillanimous – they are cowards for various reasons, but most of all it is because they do not know how to give feedback to their staff. Some men are clumsy and uncomfortable around positive feedback, but most do not know how to give negative feedback. This is now called "developmental opportunities", not "weaknesses", but it amounts to the same thing.

Managers know that people react badly to negative feedback. They demand evidence of a typical incidence that epitomized the behavior and the result is an argument about the past that neither recalls terribly well. Wiser managers deal with the problem by describing carefully the sort of behavior they want to see in the future that is specifically relevant to this particular problem. The focus is on the future not the past; on good rather than bad behavior.

Performance management systems fail if people do not receive regular, accurate feedback on their performance. It is essential for the system and your boss that he has this meeting and allows you to consider the form. You do not necessarily need a copy of it, simply an opportunity to discuss it.

You could contact HR about it but that is to react to pusillanimity with much the same. You have to help your boss be better at giving feedback. He probably needs assurance that you will not (a) break down, (b) scream and shout, (c) threaten litigation, but that you would like to know what you are doing well and how you can improve. Remember he or she probably feels inadequate and gauche. Help them and you help yourself.

Networming

What is, and what is not, a "networking opportunity"? People are bribed, invited and seduced into going to conferences and conventions, fairs and symposia, just to network. More like to "get work".

But can and should you network at dinner parties, or church gatherings? Is it OK, desirable, U or non-U, to be an opportunistic networker? Is it not just plain vulgar, bad form and brash?

And what does it entail? Do you need to go on a networking skills course? Networking means essentially building up and nurturing social contacts. Those lucky, talented or social enough to go to the "right" schools and university and go to the "best employers" simply call in their contacts they have made over time. The "old boy" network gets one into manifold clubs. They provide references, testimonials and advice.

Those who did not start lucky may find alternative routes. The one-man band or the start-up entrepreneur has to start somewhere getting to know people and building up contacts. The Rotary, The Round Table and other such organizations could be seen as ideal places to network. The golf club, the Freemasons Hall, and the IOD all provide opportunities for meeting a wide variety of potentially useful people.

Networking has now acquired the status of a desirable, even requisite business activity. It has come to be seen as a branch of marketing. It is a form of proactive personal marketing, hoping to work on personal referrals and reduce the need for cold calling.

There are apparently several steps in the networking journey and various skills to be acquired en route. The first task of course is to choose your target, that is, who to network? The question is who will help you most, when and why?

Then you have to find the right event and association. Of course it is never one event, but many. For a good list of contacts, there needs to be many ways of finding them. You may even want to categorize contacts into different groups for different purposes.

So you have your list of people and places, now it's time to do your homework. You need to know how to find them at events and what sort of people they are, what they are after.

And then you need the "Do you come here often?" starter. You are going to need that politically astute skill of getting a conversation going and then steering it to your goal. Friendly, informative, interesting, the hard sell, no vulgar pitch.

At conferences you may volunteer to talk, and/or ask intelligent questions from the floor to identify yourself. You might be asked to be placed at a particular table. And you may suggest card exchange right at the beginning so that people get to know one another.

And you have to do the Kennedy bit or at least give the impression of doing so. That is, ask not what *they* can do for *you*, but what *you* can do for *them*.

It can be a bit like speed dating. You have two or three minutes to do your thing. But there is also the follow up email, which may hopefully lead to a longer meeting.

It's easy to be cynical about the whole thing, seeing it as a false, North American device to pretend friendship when what one is doing is simply selling. But it gets worse. On networking courses people are encouraged to think of themselves as a brand. They are encouraged to dress, think and speak in accordance with a brand image they adopt. They are urged to see every social contact – the long-haul flight, the tea-after-the-service, the children's speech day, as an opportunity to grow the address book.

It can all get a bit much.

Nyet: stopping progress

The collapse of the old Soviet Union has, alas, not resulted in the end of "nyet culture". There are still many individuals who have most effectively absorbed their corporate culture and default on "No: sorry, it can't, shouldn't, will not be done". They can provide quick and effective answers as to why everything is impossible.

The nyet individual in the nyet company may be given vision-things and mission statements about creativity, innovation, customer service, responsiveness and the like, but they simply ignore them. Such employees often come from the "jobs worth" sector of society, with poor intrinsic motivation and low pay, but no performance management system.

The ideal request-stopper is short, serious and leads to an immediate end to the idea. So "too busy" or "not in my job description" or "company policy" will not do.

Is "nyetness" a stable personality trait, manifest early in life, or learnt through hard knocks? Is "potty refusal" the first sign of this syndrome (Customer Negativity Syndrome) or is it perhaps more associated with power than stubbornness? Can it be learnt by early school and job experience where role models embody everything about the syndrome? It's more likely that both personality and experience are to blame, and exercise a happy circle which is vicious to the customer, virtuous to the individual. So nyet people seek out nyet jobs in nyet organizations.

Of course there are times when all of us simply rebuff difficult, demanding requests that take up a great deal of our time and provide no benefits, only costs.

There are, however three rather good, simple, tried and tested responses to be recommended. The first is to baldly state *"for security reasons"*. This is an excellent post 9/11, post House of Commons and Buckingham Palace invasion response. We have got used to massive and sudden increases in security. Air travel is now a desperate tedious bore, but we all know why security procedures are in place and endure the consequences.

Ordinary buildings containing little of interest and value, and certainly irrelevant to national security are now controlled and patrolled by uncharmable security staff hiding their appalling boredom under a scowl. They know they have wonderful powers over the powerful. They can stop anybody and demand they show their security pass or some other means of identification.

But the "can't because of security" has the potential to be easily and happily transferred to practically anything. From where you park your car, to gaining access to any sort of information, the "can't because of security" works like a dream. If you argue back with a mix of cool logic and reasonable questions, you may be treated as an urban terrorist, happy to put the lives and welfare of the whole organization in danger. So best to back down.

The second request-stopper is an old favorite and still works well. It's the "*health and safety*" argument. This is subtly different from security and not quite as effective. It can be said in various ways depending on whether the reason-giver wants to side with or against the idea. To imply that the refusal is due to litigation in the past or the dictates of Brussels usually means the person can subtly side with the requester in spirit but lament the impossibility of anything being done.

Alternatively the request-stopper can attempt to induce guilt in the requester by suggesting that they are proposing something that is highly dangerous, unhealthy and a threat to lots of innocent people's lives, incomes, and so on. It is often useful to have handbooks and references that point out precisely what, why, where and how things should never be done.

The third request-stopper is that of the millennium and comes in many forms, the easiest of which is "*data protection*". This is a particularly good wheeze for those who are a little behind in their computer skills and are not quite sure what it all means. The idea is that anything that is electronically controlled somehow requires special access. Such people are dimly aware that information which is stored on disk is different from that stored in old manila files. They are aware of cyber-fraud and identify theft.

So anything that is associated with computers, swipe cards and the like offers the "data protection act" excuse.

The marvelous thing about the nyet trilogy is that the statements never seem to require a great deal of elaboration. They are simple and effective request and behavior stoppers. Further, they can be used in combination, so "Sorry, security and health and safety legislation" means that "under no circumstances can you" is rather good. Or try "data protection, security-based rules means that I cannot allow . . .".

Practice using the nyet trilogy! You never know when you may need them. But if you find yourself using each more than twice a week, it may be time for therapy.

Odd places: university management

Playwrights and television directors have no problems depicting universities and the people in them. They usually come in two models. The first is the benevolent view where bookish, avuncular dons potter about in booked-lined studies, drinking sherry and correcting students' and each others' grammar.

The second, from the "Look Back in Anger" school, sees academic institutions as dens of political intrigue with maverick, jealous and possibly corrupt dons stabbing each other in the back for puny prizes.

But universities do remain odd places, staffed by odd people. The way they are governed, managed and developed has surprised many a consultant. And when retiring politicians or business tycoons become involved in more ways than accepting honorary degrees or professorships (honorary, titular, special), many express surprise about the functioning of the whole enterprise.

There are several features that make university management different and make universities strange places to work in. The consequences are both positive and negative for the inmates. The first phenomenon is *managerial amateurism*. Most dons think management is either just common sense, or something easily picked up in a couple of months. Whilst a case could be made for this twenty years ago it may be less true now. This problem is made worse by the fact that most universities are run mainly by scientists. Vice chancellors are often engineers, mathematicians, physicists. Why? Most often because academics in the hard sciences peak early. Few mathematicians do their best work after the age of 40. Equally, few historians, or philosophers or linguists do their best work under 40. Middle-aged scientists, with their best years behind them, then look to the administrative roles for career and salary enhancement.

So the humanities tend to be under-represented in university management and so does humanitarianism. The way hard scientists think and are trained often makes them poor people managers. All businesses know the problem among IT and R&D specialists, among actuaries and some engineers. Their temperament, their people skills, their insight make them poor managers despite their undoubted ability. They are convergent, not divergent thinkers; they seek clear logical arguments to complex problems. And people, irrational and rational, are very complex.

Few academics are trained in management. And their attitude to training is deeply skeptical. Paradoxical really. Teachers who don't want to learn. One consequence of this is that they tend to manage as they were managed. If you have no formal training and poor role models, the problems become self-perpetuating.

Universities have very flat structures. There are very few levels (lecturer, senior lecturer, reader, professor). Most of the lecturing staff are only two or three levels below the vice chancellor (who is effectively the CEO). This makes for two problems. Dons are insensitive to rank, so people at higher levels have difficulty asserting their authority. Secondly, the reporting structure is both unmanageable and unclear. Most dons have never been asked the simple question "To whom do you report?" They haven't the slightest idea. But if they do, given the very flat nature of the organization, it may be that fifty or so in a big department report to one person. The simple span-of-control idea, a Weberian concept, goes out of the window. Nobody can manage fifty direct reports, particularly if they are maverick dons.

Another curious feature of the academic world is reliance on peer review. This means that a person's promotion depends on people around the world whom he or she may never have met. Hence the importance of publications and reputation. Thus if your boss recommends you for promotion as a result of your hard work, dedication and ability, yet a few researchers on the other side of the world "blackball" you, that is that. The peer review system therefore puts heavy reliance on networking rather than loyalty to the department and university.

Universities have always enjoyed secrecy. There is a pervasive culture of non-openness. This extends to knowing how much people are paid for comparative workloads. There are both benefits and drawbacks of this. It reduces jealousy but increases paranoia.

Universities have very powerful central control. There is often little diffusion of responsibility, financial control and the like. This means that "Peter is robbed to pay Paul". Less successful departments are subsidized by more successful ones. Fair enough you might say, but the problem is confounded by power, wealth and reputation. Thus media studies (a lowly discipline) might subsidize physics (a highly rated discipline). Sports science may be taxed to pay for Fine Arts. Economics may have to double enrolment to bail out chemistry.

So dons receive conflicting messages about being entrepreneurial, self-sufficient and so on, when they find their efforts are in reality highly controlled.

The final straw is government intervention and meddling. Perfectly OK you might argue, because, after all, most university income comes from teaching. Governments legislate for "better management". Staff need regular appraisal, lectures should be assessed. But they also attempt social engineering. Particular groups are to be selected because of their demography, not their ability.

People learn about management in two ways: through the experience of being managed (well or otherwise) and through formal training and instruction. Most dons feel training courses are below them. They often have also experienced only amateur, reluctant or downright incompetent managers. No wonder then that universities are odd places completely immune to management science.

Orality at work

Freudian ideas and concepts have amazed, influenced and shocked for over a hundred years. Psychology students still thrill to the counter-intuitive explanations and supposedly powerful force of the unconscious. Writers and artists (but few scientists) have been profoundly influenced by the ideas of old Sigmund and his followers.

And over the past hundred years many of his ideas and language has bubbled down into everyday language. Though they might not fully understand the terms, people happily talk about anal obsessionality, penis envy and oedipal conflicts. They are usually amazed by the labels – nearly always used pejoratively – that mixes wickedness and perversion.

But psychoanalysis is more than a set of curious terms and labels. It purports to describe and explain individual differences. But Freudians rarely use questionnaires to assess personality. They believe that people cannot, as opposed to will not, tell you what really motivates them. Dark, contradictory, unconscious forces are the real drivers.

Freudians also believe that adult personality bears the scars of childhood experiences. Most laypeople know about the trauma of the potty and how this leads to anal obsessive behavior. But they appear to know less about the earlier phase of psychosexual development and the scars it can cause. It is called the oral phase and it is all about the trauma of weaning.

According to the theory, fortunately most of us pass through the phase happily. But some don't: those weaned too early and those too late. Both become oral: but some *oral optimists* and others *oral pessimists*. The latter throughout life find the mouth and all oral activities a source of pleasure (even eroticism). So, eating, drinking, talking, singing and smoking are a joy. As is playing wind instruments and kissing.

So one may expect oral optimists to become opera singers and wine tasters, radio presenters and motivational speakers.

On the other hand we have those weaned dramatically and early. They are oral pessimists. They seem to thrive on sarcasm and are argumentative. They are oral sadists using the mouth to spit venom, give biting comments, return ideas well chewed over. So according to the theory they become dentists and lawyers. They bite their nails and pencils. They enjoy malicious gossip.

Oral people of course get fussy with food. And there is research to show that food preference is related to oral type. So oral pessimists like hot, biting food: a meat Madras, preserved ginger, sherbet. The gregarious oral optimists like rice pudding, milky, mashed potato. Of course we know that other factors like culture influence food preferences.

But the idea is an interesting one. Many aspects of our personality are influenced by long-forgotten and repressed ideas and experiences. They determine in later life, at least in part, our job choices and hobbies. They explain why we get satisfaction from some activities and not others.

Why would anyone want to become a dentist? Good pay, professional respectability? Well, partly, but also to enact one's oral sadism. And what about a barrister: the money of course, the life style, the fame? Yes, but also the joy of vicious interrogation, of publicly displayed bitter-sweet irony and of talking your way to wealth.

The claptrap of a long-dead Austrian psychiatrist or the insights of one of the greatest thinkers of the nineteenth century? Discuss.

Organizational defense mechanisms

Anna Freud, daughter of her famous bearded Moravian father, also made her own contributions to psychology. She is well known for developing various ideas. One of the most famous is describing *ego mechanisms of defense.*

The idea is this. We all develop, over time, ways of protecting and defending our (brittle) ego against threat and attack. We have to learn to deal with setback and failure, humiliation and disappointment and the terrible realization that (alas) we can't always get what we want. We are vulnerable, fragile and mortal.

In Freudian terms we have to balance the quite irrational and irrepressible needs of the totally pleasure seeking *id* with the powerful morally disapproving *superego* or conscience. The *ego* is at the heart of the battle of this curious triumvirate. Hence ego defenses.

The Freudians spent much effort spelling out some of these typical defense mechanisms some of which are very familiar: denial, repression, regression. Others are a bit more, well, Freudian, like projection, introjection and reaction formation. Different writers come up with slightly different nomenclature but there is usually an agreed list.

The idea is that individuals "choose" their own particular armory of preferred defense mechanisms. Some are more primitive than others. Indeed it may be that they are a good index of both pathology and ability. Thus rigid obsessionals favor one mechanism and hysterical flibbertigibbets another. *Developmentalists* are concerned with how defense mechanisms develop and why some individuals appear to prefer or use some over others. *Sociologists* are interested in this distribution in the population as a whole. *Anthropologists* wonder if they differ from culture to culture.

But *management-ologists* interested in corporate culture have noted how the personal preferences of single individuals (frequently company founders) often shape acceptable (and unacceptable) forms of behavior in the workplace. Corporate culture, the "way we do things round here", may be shaped by below-the-surface values, but pretty soon new employees begin to absorb, imitate and repeat the accepted forms of behavior, from dress codes and forms of address to timekeeping.

It is possible that organizations themselves sanction defense mechanisms. That is, it may become pro- and prescribed to behave in particular ways when the corporate ego is threatened. Consider the mechanisms and how they "play out" in business life:

- **Repression:** This is an unconscious mechanism that keeps thoughts and memories that are too threatening out of awareness. Many organizations are amnesic about the past. Stories about immoral, illegal, or just plain stupid behavior are repressed. Often so much so that forgetting the past leads to repetition.

- **Denial:** This is the refusal to acknowledge external realities and/or emotions. People often say about themselves and others that they are "in denial". But it can become an organizational craze: denial about the anger of customers, the anxiety of shareholders, the short-termism of the current strategy.

- **Projection:** This is the attribution of personal unacknowledged and unacceptable impulses to others. Thus you may have a tad too much greed and dubious ethical practices, or too little moral fiber and concern for others. So these bad qualities are projected on to a "bad" object – ideally, one's competitors, but other possibilities include politicians, regulators or even suppliers.

- **Reaction-formation:** This is the strategy of turning unacceptable feelings into their opposites. Thus an unconscious repulsion for something can be expressed as delight, fascination or a deep need for it. This is more than hypocrisy. It is a powerful rejection of ideas, preferences, approaches to delicate policy areas, such as equal opportunities, maternity leave and trade unions.

- **Sublimation:** This is the converting of problematic impulses, often about sex and aggression, into socialized activities. So highly competitive, pathologically ambitious managers may in fact be in real competition with their siblings, even father. The spinster who works with children is sublimating as is the manager who wants to run a crèche.

- **Rationalization:** The preferred defense of the articulate and educated. It is the explanation of unacceptable feelings of guilt, shame and the like. It may require elaborate casuistical *ethical codes* about ends justifying mean; *psychobabble* explaining away incompetence or immorality, or quasi *legal babble* which insists on reasonable courses of action in the circumstances.

- **Displacement:** Coming home and kicking the cat, slapping the kids and shouting at the spouse may be classic displacement. It is the shifting of acceptable feelings (being angry with a fickle indolent employee) from one person to another. Very bad when customers find themselves on the receiving end of senior management disgruntlement.

- **Regression:** This is behaving in a way characteristic of a previous developmental level, often petulant and adolescent-like.

Passive–aggressive bureaucrats

Passive–Aggressive Personalities (PAP) are often talked about by laypeople. Many are found in administrative jobs and, boy, can they frustrate one. They are experts on contrariness. And they constantly complain, deliberately dawdle, frequently "forget", often oppose, and sulkily stall. They feel cheated and deprived but being scornful helps.

PAPs are often preoccupied with their own goals and dreams. They resent being disturbed or interrupted. Although requests for greater focus, openness, productivity, or effort will irritate them, they do not express their irritation directly; rather, they will express it in relatively subtle ways. Hence the passive–aggressive bit.

They are often late for meetings, they procrastinate, and they put off working on tasks that don't interest them. They blame their non-performance on computer failures, lack of adequate resources, lack of cooperation from someone else, being poorly managed, or failure to be given clear instruction. As managers they tend to set up their staff for failure by not telling them what they want, and then criticizing them for not delivering what they allege they actually wanted.

And, for customers, dealing with them is, to say the least, a challenge. The more power they have the less customer oriented they are.

There are two takes on the PAP. The first is that they simply have not learnt enough social skills. They do not know how to be assertive. The assertive person is someone able to communicate their desires, feelings and thoughts in ways that do not violate the rights of others. They can easily and effectively communicate wants, dislikes and feelings in a clear, direct manner without being rude or threatening. They are candid but have consideration for others.

The PAP is not like this. They are not candid about their motives and often find subtle ways to convey their reactions and feelings. And they also tend to be subversive and unconcerned about those they deal with.

The optimist believes that with a bit of training the PAP can be taught the skills of assertiveness. They can learn to identify, regulate and express their emotions and those of others. And they can be "grown up", polite and helpful in dealing with stress.

The other take is rather more depressing and serious. It sees PAPs as people with a serious personality disorder. The psychiatric manual specifies nine recognizable characteristics of the PAP:

1. They procrastinate all the time. Deadlines are not met frequently.
2. They become sulky, irritable, or argumentative when asked to do something they do not want to do. This occurs frequently at work.
3. They seem to work deliberately slowly or to do a bad job on tasks they really do not want to do. That is, they sabotage all tasks they resent doing. And there are quite a few.
4. They protest, without much justification, that others make unreasonable demands on them. This is often done subtly, anonymously but constantly.
5. They avoid obligations by claiming to have "forgotten" to the extent some might be thought to have a serious brain disorder.
6. They believe that they do a much better job than others think they do. Information given at appraisals and 360-degree feedback is often a rude shock.
7. They resent useful suggestions from others concerning how they could be more productive. In this sense they are very difficult to manage.
8. They regularly obstruct the efforts of others by failing to do their share of the work. They are a nightmare in a team.
9. They unreasonably criticize or scorn people in positions of authority, both in and out of the organization.

Recognize the above? Alas, so many people do that the very latest psychiatric diagnostic manuals have dropped this disorder from the list. They argue that PAP behavior appears too frequently in the population for it to be a serious psychiatric disorder. But when they do they can drive others crazy with swings of contrition and evasiveness, hubris and humility, impudence and oleaginousness.

Sometimes, very cautious people are misclassified. Others believe some forms of PA behavior are a reaction to arbitrary, unreasonable conformity pressure.

PAPS are neither happy in themselves, nor easy to deal with. They make demands which you have to learn to resist assertively and in doing so provide a model of what you want. They are not very sensitive to your needs, so you have to spell them out clearly and frequently. They are stubborn and very sensitive to their rights. So ask them what it is that you have to do in order to get them to do what you want.

Confront them when they stall, forget or refuse. Say you feel they are angry and need to talk about it. They are people without much pleasure and respond well and dramatically to a compliment.

But there is a crumb of comfort if you work for a PAP or have to deal with one as a colleague or customer. They experience frequent capping or downward job mobility. That is, they rarely reach positions of real power.

The personality of organizations

Marketing types love to talk about "brand personality". They mean quite simply a set of characteristics or traits associated with a particular brand.

This is not, of course, to anthromorphize brands or organizations. They do not have personalities but they do have a social image, a reputation. The idea is that we think about organizations in people terms. We think of cars and hotels, of restaurants and cinemas in people terms. We use the 36,000 trait words in the English language.

We derive our impressions of brand personality from advertisements, personal experience and the experience of others. Organizations are often symbols, icons, representatives of value sets. But we use trait adjectives to describe them and hence the idea of brand personality.

So brands or organizations can be seen as "sincere" or "exciting" or (just plain) "competent". They may also be "sophisticated" or "rugged".

For nearly fifty years marketing people have asked consumers to rate organizations on all kinds of dimensions. One recent American study (published this year in the *Journal of Applied Psychology*) asked people to rate familiar organizations (Microsoft, Nike, Disney, etc., and so on) using trait words. And from this analysis they found evidence of five types of organizations.

The first they called *Boy Scout*. They were seen as being friendly, family oriented, pleasant, personal, helpful, honest, cooperating, clean, and so on. The sort of virtues Baden-Powell promoted and were very desirable.

The second type were *Innovative*. They were characterized by being creative, exciting, interesting, unique and original. The third were characterized in terms of their *Dominance*. They were big, busy, successful and popular.

The fourth had a positive label but somewhat pejorative characteristics. They were thought of in terms of *Thrift* but this meant simple, sloppy and lower class. The final personality type was referred to in terms of *Style*. Organizations in this group were modern, contemporary and trendy.

Most of the personality types were associated with consistent positive traits. Boy Scout, Innovative and Stylish were uniformly good. But Dominant organizations could be seen as bullying and demanding while Thrift organizations are often seen as sloppy, disorganized and deprived.

But so what? Is this just marketing types having fun? Perhaps, but organizational personalities do affect consumers – and future job applicants. In the study, the researchers got people both to rate organizations and to specify three other things: how attractive the company appeared to be as a place to work; their future intentions toward the company as a place to work or shop; and their perception of the company's reputation.

The results were pretty clear. People loved Boy Scout organizations most, followed by Stylish, then Innovative. Overall, Dominance was good. And they really didn't like Thrift organizations at all.

It is quite clear that organizations are marketed in terms of their behavioral traits. We have "listening banks" and "rock-bottom price" warehouses.

The question is what sort of organizations do we prefer? Do we want our supermarket Stylish or Thrifty or a bit Boy Scout?

And the same applies to the public sector. All public sector organizations, from one's local library to the local college, have a personality. Some spend vast sums of money trying to be different. You attract *young* people by being innovative and attract *classy* people by having style, *poor* people through thrift, *successful* people with dominance . . . or do you?

The brand personality concept certainly helps one do joined-up marketing, planning and staffing.

Professional recruiters

It's amusing to make fun of train and plane spotters. Seen en masse at airports or conventions, people with passions – be they for bird species or steam engines, vintage cars or postage stamps, war memorabilia or exotic snakes – can seem very odd indeed.

Certainly with some enthusiasms, the followers (or addicts or victims) are surprisingly demographically similar. Your average plane spotter is a 42-year-old, modestly educated, introverted man. Compared to the population norms their levels of job-related social skills might be surprisingly different. And so is their personality profile.

One hears the shrill cry of "stereotypic prejudice"; of seeing uniform homogeneity where heterogeneity exists; of being an ignorant smirking outsider with little or no understanding of the people, their passion or proclivities.

But it is true that if you were able to rustle up a hundred very successful accountants or architects, priests or publicans, soldiers or sales staff, you would be struck as much by their similarities as by their differences.

Indeed this is the basis of the *known-groups method* in vocational guidance. It consists of finding a large group of adjusted, happy and successful people in a particular job and tracing those factors they have in common (beliefs, abilities, personality) that drew them to both the job *and* being successful in it. These similarities then form the basis of the selection criteria.

Often enthusiasts say they can spot each other. They "know" when they have met a member of the clan.

And this phenomenon has serious implications for all job selection. Given that those in the job are perhaps the best to spot those with the "right" attitudes, aptitudes and traits, why employ professional HR recruiters and selectors?

Consider the following example. Some jobs, yes even important jobs, are best suited to introverted, rule-following types who seem tolerant of boredom: in stores maintenance, long-distance lorry driving, as dental technicians, proofreaders.

These "types" seldom interview well. They can be stiff, monosyllabic, highly literal. They usually hate the selection process in the first place.

But recruiters have been attracted to their job because they are sociable, inquisitive, quirky. They are often party animals – extroverted, impulsive, fun loving. And they, as do we, all too often select in their own image. If you like

"MBTI speak" it's ENFPs selecting INTJs. Or, if you like NEO-PI talk, it's Open-to-Experience extroverts choosing Practical, Focused Introverts.

The problem with interviews is precisely that they tend to override highly sensible work done on job analysis or wisely chosen personality profiling. Some people just seem more likeable than others. And shy "anoraks" don't fare well – except of course among their own.

Not all successful job-holders have as much insight as others. But those bright enough to climb the greasy pole have had their fair share of success and failure enough to have learnt from experience. And they might really know the signs – of both success and failure. They know what to look for, even if they might need training in interview technique. They can be taught how to elicit the information they need and to brush up their social skills. They know panel interviewing usually makes things worse not better – less reliable and less valid. There is competition for good people: that is why you need professional interviewers.

In the ideal world the experienced and professional interviewer starts with a comprehensive job analysis: indeed, a career analysis. The aim is to be able to describe the full set of traits, abilities and values a successful job-holder needs. And then to find them via questionnaire or biodata or interviews. Charming, attractive, jovial interviewees do, but should not, have an advantage, unless these characteristics are terribly relevant to the job. Sure there are many jobs where these traits are crucial, many where they are helpful but lots and lots where they make no difference at all.

Protecting your legacy

Powerful people of a certain age and at a certain stage often ponder their legacy. What will they leave behind? How will history remember them? And, indeed, what can they do now to ensure a favorable mark in posterity?

Do senior people sometimes take their eye off the ball as a result of being too concerned with their legacy and so, paradoxically and ironically, destroy it?

People do very strange things to try to influence history. Some try to destroy all their papers so no record is left. Others selectively remove, edit and insert forged documents to try to confuse historians of the future. Some spend lavishly to buy forgiveness in their later years for what passed in earlier times. Others search for biographers "deeply sympathetic" to their side of the story.

Those who, like all of us, seek to "live on" but have the means to do so usually try various methods.

The first is *philanthropical*: donate money to a cause. Educational institutions always seem worthy recipients. The very successful businessman Lord Wolfson had colleges named after him at both Oxford and Cambridge being the only person apart from Jesus Christ to have this honor. Sometimes you simply give away money at the rate and speed that you made it, hoping that the parable about the camel, the eye of the needle and heaven will then not apply.

Even if you are not wealthy, a charitable foundation can be started. Here one thinks of the Cheshire Homes where a famous fighter ace dedicated his long life to saving rather than killing people. But this is usually a life-long quest, not simply a pre-retirement activity.

Another possible legacy is something *physical*: perhaps the pyramids are the most dramatic example. The idea is to have a physical monument: a great library (think of recent American presidents) bearing one's name, a folly perhaps, a grand house. Hadrian is remembered for his wall – and little else.

A third method is *legal*: this is an attempt to introduce an eponymous law that will create more justice. William Wilberforce is remembered for stopping slavery. But this method is very difficult unless you are a politician.

Another method is to *write*: plays, books, poems, or indeed the modern equivalent – producing films or TV programmes. The trouble with this method is that it takes both time and talent.

What happens to CEOs when their thoughts turn to their real or likely or desirable legacy? What is it they want history to say of them: they were just and kind? They turned things around? They had both courage and wisdom?

Occasionally on training courses for serious grown-ups the instructors ask people to write their own obituary. This is not meant to examine writing ability or indeed to prove one can still remember what one has done. The real reason is to look back and note real achievements: those that others recognize and will last. In this task scribblers often lurch between hubris and humility, both of which are inappropriate. The lesson is to sort the wheat from the chaff: to distinguish the transient from the long lasting, the real achievements vs the trivial.

It is said that Nobel (he of the prizes) having read his own obituary, which was of course an error, decided to give all his money away. He did not want to be remembered for having made a fortune from explosives. Rather he wanted his name associated with great discoveries in science, great literature, and peace, not war.

There is a real danger that these legacy dreams and plans influence the present. A CEO is responsible to many shareholders. It is the CEO's job to ensure the business is viable, productive and profitable. And that it weathers the storm of globalization and the turbulence of the stockmarket. The best strategy is to concentrate on that with energy and passion. That in itself is legacy enough.

A psychological MOT

"Rust and decay in all around I see, Oh Lord who changest not abide with me". Indeed. Old cars, indeed all machinery breaks down. Granted, not as much as it used to. In fact we now appear to throw away perfectly functional but out-of-date or strangely incompatible machinery long before its natural life is over.

And maybe that's a useful metaphor for people at work. Some are made redundant while in perfect working order. Others wear out, break down, potter on at half power – half working.

For cars, we wisely require owners to take them for an annual check-up. Cars need a certificate of road-worthiness. A mechanic goes over the car, we trust with a fine toothcomb detecting that which is not working; that which is on-the-edge; and that which is past its sell-by, guarantee date. This check reduces the chance of the car malfunctioning and accidents occurring. Sensible strategy.

The same principle applies to particular jobs. Thus aeroplane pilots have to undergo a rigorous physical check-up to ensure they are fit to fly. Simple but significant markers like blood pressure help predict the likelihood that a pilot might be taken seriously ill while in command of a plane.

It's the same principle with loyalty. Every so often those working for organizations trusted with state secrets are re-interviewed to go over their value system and political beliefs. People can be compromised by all the old favorites: sex, money, drugs. They can be "turned" by feeling they are scorned or belittled. And they can then find it easy enough to dance with the devil, spill the beans and act treacherously.

But what about the mental health of senior executives? These days every psychiatric disorder appears to have its own self-help group and website. Most are at pains to describe what is known about the disorder. And they often give surprising statistics on the number of people in the population who suffer from it. This is just as true of the serious psychotic disorders (Schizophrenia, Manic–Depressive Illness), through the problematic personality disorders (Psychopathy, Narcissism), to the better known neurotic disorders (Phobia, Depression, Anxiety, Panic Attacks).

Most big organizations have some employees with addictions. What is interesting and telling is how they respond to someone with a serious drinking or drug problem. Too many turn a blind eye until some spectacular event forces them to act.

But what about board members who have lost the plot? What about a one-ulcer manager holding down a two-ulcer board position? What about the five-years-off-early-retirement director who has not and will not master the technology for the new age?

There is usually a delicate fudge between the concept of a *development* center and an *assessment* center. Assessment centers are expensive, intensive but effective ways of obtaining important information about individuals in the selection process. Candidates are closely observed and measured on many real-task simulations to see how they perform. Abilities, values, even social skills are rated in group-work exercises.

Development centers are much the same except they are supposed to have a quite different aim. That is to take what one has got and improve it. To develop people to realize their potential, maximize their strengths, explore their talents. It is supposedly as much about attitude as ability; about mental health and outlook as mastering specific skills.

And this may be (or already is) the ideal time to conduct an executive MOT on senior managers. They are assessed, appraised, evaluated by trained outsiders – psychologists and the like – to judge their work style, their coping strategy, their hardiness. It's not uncommon to find serious pathology in the boardroom. Some believe cynically it is the only way of getting there.

Rank sensitivity

Most organizations are endeavoring to become flatter. The old Weberian idea of maximum span-of-control has been jettisoned except perhaps in the army. The idea was that no one leader/manager could possibly manage or lead more than seven (plus or minus two) people. So rank was logically and arithmetically and simply a function of a statistical formula.

Span-of-control organizations are deeply sensitive to rank. As are many corporate and national cultures in general. We used to call it "respect for authority". Etiquette books still tell one precisely how to address a Duke as opposed to a Viscount, an Archbishop to an Archdeacon. And those curious almost medieval niceties extend to the order of titles. So one is Professor Sir Adrian, but the Reverend Colonel Ellis. Charming? Old fashioned? Utterly irrelevant? The opposite of Cool Britannia. No – just evidence of a power distant culture with sensitivity to rank.

The story is thus: over the years researchers have tried to discover and then describe the basic fundamental dimensions of national culture. One of those is sensitivity to rank. Countries, corporations and individuals differ on this feature. It has also been called power distance. And it has consequences.

Globe-trotters notice national culture rank-sensitivity. In many parts of Asia, like India, Japan and the Philippines, people are very observant with respect to rank and status. Most of us know about the depth of the bow in Japan being a clear sign of rank of both parties.

Equally in the equalitarian Nordic countries it is often very difficult to differentiate rank and power in groups.

Rank and status is related to many things. Simple demographics like age and sex still dictate who "gives way", when and how. But education, profession, and various social connections are even more important. One can have rank and status by personal achievements or by family background. One is earned, the other inherited. One can be a life peer or a hereditary one.

If the organization is flat (as in a university) people are aware of titles but rarely use them to each other. People gain the respect of all (technically superiors, peers and subordinates) by their knowledge and job performance. And senior jobs are populated by very diverse people in terms of their backgrounds.

But in hierarchical rank-sensitive organizations, titles are used extensively and the top people are at least traditionally middle-aged, pale males. Respect is obtained by service and commitment.

Rank-sensitive organizations tend to favor greater centralization and more supervisors. They openly value white- over blue-collar jobs. They are sensitive to power: who has it, how it is obtained, how it is used.

If you come from a flat organization (a consultancy) and want to deal with a tall one, get out your wrinklies to impress them that you are serious. Pay respect, however incompetent a senior person you come across; never publicly belittle them. Give yourself a grand title (Senior Vice President is a sure winner). And don't challenge too much.

On the other hand if *you* are tall and *they* are flat remember they are usually impressed by ability, knowledge and skill. Respond to their ability not their influence, rank or power. Feel free to criticize and challenge: that is a good sign in flat organizations.

The problem is this: fad, fashion and zeitgeist dictate that organizations are now flattened, de-levelled, with fewer ranks. But changing culture is neither easy nor always desirable. Is it possible to optimally structure the organization to suit the task? One manager cannot properly and effectively manage fifty people.

It is where the structure does not fit the primary organizational structure and process that one has problems. And remember when trying to flatten organizations greatest resistance comes from the top where there is most power. If you propose to be a trendy leveller expect entrenched resistance.

Recruitment to betrayal

Organizations are increasingly sensitive to employees who lie, steal and sabotage their company in one way or another. They wonder how or why they went wrong in recruitment and selection. And they flirt with the idea of integrity tests, even the quasi-scientific polygraph (lie detector).

Most organizations are convinced that those who betray them in one way or another are rotten apples in the barrel, maverick psychopaths or amoral loonies. Few even entertain the possibility that they are the cause of this behavior. The very idea that they recruit reasonably moral, upstanding people and somehow turn them into the enemy within seems utterly preposterous. And yet case histories suggest that much betrayal is organization-born.

Consider the issue of integrity. This is about honesty and truthfulness. It is about having a strong moral compass, informed by an accepted ethical code. So where and when do the lies begin?

Let's start with recruitment fairs and job advertisements. Ask anyone who works in and for a company to "deconstruct" their recruitment blurb. Does it present a realistic picture of the job? What does "challenging" really mean? What is left out? Consider the corporate video. An advertisement like any other. The best buildings, happy staff, supportive colleagues, delighted customers. Cloud-cuckoo-land.

But everyone does it. No one presents the bland bald truth about themselves in the press or during the student milk-round. That is as may be, but there is a distinction to be made between exaggeration, falsehood and downright lies.

And then there is the selection procedure. Candidates are frequently accused of false presentational devices and impression management. They put on their best suit, their best persona and rehearse their best answers. True. But it is not a one-way street.

Selectors too are in the presentation business. They answer as well as ask questions. They provide packs of details to the applicant. They too put on their best front. They promise, they seduce, they obfuscate.

So a successful job candidate risks the possibility that all the information he or she has been given at recruitment and selection bears only a quasi-approximation to the truth.

The next stage is induction if there is one. Once again, this is a rah-rah occasion of celebration, fun, heroics – and half truths. Again, it can be deeply misleading. Some candidates are treated as contestant winners. Rarely do they receive a balanced view of (really) how things are.

So it can be a rude shock once the partying is over to confront the real thing. Lazy, bullying, incompetent managers; alienated, backstabbing, unsupported peers; hyper-demanding, deeply ungrateful, excessively fickle staff.

But perhaps the world-weary job applicant should expect all this. They may be disillusioned, disappointed and disenchanted, but they are unlikely to be saboteurs, Luddites or whistle-blowers at this stage.

People, it is said, join organizations but leave managers. It need only take one or two seriously incompetent, ignorant or devious (deviant?) managers to turn an individual around. Fickle, vindictive, demanding managers may not be the norm but they exist. Often they have got away with it by skillful upward management. They identify their major "constituencies" and play to their foibles. They charm senior managers and major account handlers and dump on their reports. Like the buildings they work in, facadism is all.

So the reasonable employee is stressed, bullied, lied to and ignored. He or she sees corruption, inequity and hypocrisy all around.

People are driven to betray their companies for many reasons. Some are, as John Major called them, bastards. But most are turned. They feel vengeful, lied to, abused. Some, perhaps most, rightly so. Some get up to jolly scams to keep their jobs but work less hard. They are the quit-but-stay, frequently absent, deeply alienated workers. Their psychological contract is in shreds. Management lies, propaganda and broken promises are the origin of their betrayal, not their dubious ethics or morals.

A rock and a hard place

In these politically correct and litigious times, those simply trying to select and appoint good staff face increasing problems. Damned if they do and damned if they don't use certain procedures.

Read the recent psychological literature and the dilemma is apparent. Consider the following two very well established facts. Cognitive ability (that is, intelligence) tests are the single best predictor of an individual's job performance. More so at higher level and with very complex jobs. But it is has been consistently shown that these tests have a substantial negative impact on the employment of people from particular racial or ethnic groups. Certain groups tend to score quite a bit lower than others and therefore do not pass the selection criteria.

This is the efficiency vs equity debate. It is a clash of values. There are no easy ways out. You can't easily hide and must put your cards on the table.

The efficiency argument goes like this. Considering especially profit-making organizations, the case is that the organization is in business to make money. It is there to satisfy all stakeholders (customers, staff, shareholders, and so on) and to be lean and mean, adaptable and innovative, efficient and effective as much as possible. If people are one's most important (or even pretty important) asset, then finding and retaining the best people seems crucial. Although it is easy to make selection errors, it is important to establish characteristics of individuals that help us make better decisions with regard to selecting in or selecting out particular individuals.

There is a large body of good-quality (disinterested, scientific) research that shows cognitive ability is unique in terms of its power and relevance in predicting job performance over a wide range of jobs over the lifespan. Therefore you should test job applicants and select the top scorers, providing of course they also match other (less powerful) known criteria. It behooves any successful company to choose the brightest and the best to maximize its mission to be successful. The shareholders expect it; the markets expect it; the mission statement implies it. It is simple common sense. I rest my case for the efficiency argument, m'lud.

But what of the other side? The equity argument goes like this. Cognitive ability tests appear to have other uniquely powerful features namely their ability to discriminate against certain race groups. In America this means Blacks and Hispanics. A cheaper, non-researched and non-evidenced approach leads this camp to deny, downgrade or denigrate the data which suggest that intelligence tests are useful predictors of performance.

Using these tests (there are many to choose from) therefore means that scrupulous business decision makers are bound to discriminate on the basis of race. Further, it is also well known that racial differences in intelligence test scores are much larger than measures of job performance. Thus a workforce based on actual measured and aggregated job performance would be less racially segregated than a workforce selected on the basis of tests. This may be thought illegal, immoral and antithetical to the mission statement. In our modern multiracial society we cannot and should not ever allow tests to be used knowing that they discriminate between people. I rest my (moral) case, m'lud.

This problem has attracted those trying to find a solution. Attempts have been made to devise tests that both do not discriminate but do predict performance. They have not been successful. Others have tried to change the testing method. Another popular solution is to have different cut-off points for different groups but this does not solve the efficiency issue.

One returns to a clash of values. There are no easy solutions. One can trade-off efficiency over equity and examine the costs but then the moral, value-laden decision has to be made. Some want to put effort and time into finding non-cognitive tests that predict job performance as well. A search for the Holy Grail or a serious scientific project?

Some researchers have argued that combining the best non-cognitive tests together (that is, job knowledge, conscientiousness, integrity) may do (nearly) as well in predicting job success. But what are those other tests and don't they also discriminate in subtly different ways?

Tests, of course, are meant to discriminate, though the preferred word is probably differentiate. Discriminate means make a judgement about some quality or qualities. Wine tasters discriminate; theatre critics discriminate; book publishers discriminate. The question is, on which criteria?

The efficiency–equity problem requires one to make value judgements, even if expressed in terms of trade-off. Thus, would you prefer a selection system which leads to a productivity increase of £20,000 per annum and a 5% decrease in minority group members; or one that ensures a £2,000 increase and no reduction in minority group selection?

Values arouse passions. Good evidence is trivialized and distorted. And many duck under the parapet of fudge and spin. A good case could be made to organizational stakeholders from both camps. But it takes the brave and wise to make value-based decisions explicit and public.

Seeking the savior

The war for talent is raging. The talented wunderkind of the future are in short supply. We need them desperately – or so it is said.

So money is thrown at the goal which is to find, recruit and retain the entrepreneurial, business-savvy, emotionally intelligent, bright young things of the future. They are, it is believed, the future leaders. The hope of the organization. Carriers of the flame. Saviors of the peoples.

They are often portrayed as somewhere between Winston Churchill and John Wayne, Mother Theresa and Margaret Thatcher, Boedicea and Bismark.

What makes them so valuable is that they are exceptional. More than that they are fired by the "mission vision-thing". They are intrinsically motivated. Their whole life is dedicated to one mission, one goal, and fortunately you are a major beneficiary.

But where do they come from? And how do you find them? Are they not the rarest of beasts? Worthy of the hunt?

Alas finding them may be more like the search for the Holy Grail. Endless, exhausting and ultimately unsuccessful. At least the seekers for the Grail knew exactly what they were looking for, even if they were not sure of its exact form. The trouble with wunderkind-hunting is that it is not clear who they are, what they look like and where to find them.

Should you trawl only the best universities and have talent scouts in business schools? Or is it better to look for early signs of creative entrepreneurship in schools?

Most importantly what are the markers of the future high-flyers? Do they have to be super bright or just bright enough? And if the latter, what is the cut-off point? What about their temperament – stable, extroverts? And what of their biography – what if they come from a broken home or are second-generation immigrants: is that good or bad?

Is rebelliousness at school age a good or bad sign of later leadership? And what of living abroad, or how they spent their first salary cheque? The answer is, "We do not know".

But we are perhaps better at spotting impostors: the false messiah, those who looked like the real thing but aren't. Surprisingly few organizations have a good "select out" factor – that is, they don't actively search for criteria that should be used to exclude individuals. And they certainly learn, to their cost, the folly of not being as clear as they should be about the characteristics they don't want to have in their hires.

The good-looking, intelligent, narcissistic and psychopathic have often been hailed in their time as saviors. Their easy confidence, their guilt-free courage, their determination can be enchanting. They know what people want to hear. They flatter (and demand flattery) and their little foibles are forgiven and forgotten. Indeed such peccadilloes may even be thought of as an index of their genius. But alas it can be tears before bedtime.

Wunderkinds? Perhaps. Occasionally. But possibly the game is worth more than the candle. Maybe, just maybe, ordinary people can do extra-ordinary things if properly managed. It is better to maximize your existing talent than search for the Holy Grail. Ordinariness can disguise genius. We know from the history of war that real courage is often found in strange places. "Cometh the hour, cometh the man".

And what is wrong with promotion from within? It can increase corporate loyalty, reduce talent turnover and have other beneficial knock-on effects on the corporate culture.

So stop casting around for wunderkinds. Grow your own. It's cheaper and much more fun.

Shift work

We have conquered the night. The last shopping frontier is in the hands of our forces. We live in a 24-hour society. Supermarkets and shops of all sorts are open all hours.

We have not towns that never sleep but societies that never sleep. Fine for the shopper, the customer, the browser. Less pleasant for the shift worker, and shift work is on the increase by necessity.

There have of course always been shift workers in hospitals, power stations, on board ships, and so on. For all sorts of reasons, various people have sought out shift work because it fits into their work–life balance. But more and more people find they are going on to shift work, often involuntarily. And it may bring long and short term negative consequences.

We are a diurnal species who live on a rhythmic planet. We have developed circadian rhythms which mean even though we may be thought of as larks or owls most of us sleep at night and are active in one form or other during the day. In short, it is not natural to work at night. Our circadian clock regulates a variety of sophisticated body cycles, including temperature, hormones and heart rate.

And some shifts are particularly gruelling, as anyone who works them finds out. We are designed to sleep 11.00 pm to 7.00 am. Shifts differ greatly in their type, length and number. And of course so does work. Packing supermarket shelves at 02.00 am is different from monitoring power-station computers, which is different again from working in hospital accident and emergency wards. Driving a taxi at night again is quite a different affair.

The problems lie essentially in the sleep problems that result from shift work. These can be both chronic and acute. And the story is pretty familiar. Shift work leads to sleep problems which lead to tiredness which in turn leads to the all-familiar work outcomes: absenteeism, accidents, higher dissatisfaction and job turnover but lower morale and productivity. The tired, sleep-deprived worker is quite irritable, impatient and unhelpful. They can become mentally and physically sick.

Daytime sleep is quite simply more disturbed, shorter and truncated. There is good sleep and bad sleep. The former is deep (REM) dreaming sleep, the latter shallow. If you don't get enough of the former, it has an effect. People concentrate less well, even "nod off" on the job, having necessary but involuntary and unplanned sleeps.

How to minimize the build-up of sleep-deprived fatigue? You could abolish the evening shift, but that is simply not possible in many jobs. Or try to select people with lots of shift-work experience who appear to be immune to its effects – perhaps even thriving on them. This too is problematic as shift work is on the increase, with as many as 25% of workers on shift work.

The only other sensible suggestion is to redesign jobs and train workers. One approach is to try to minimize long middle-of-the-night shifts but the more obvious alternative is to introduce compulsory, specific rest breaks with recommendations and training with regard to what to do in them.

Shift workers have to be trained to sleep better. Most of us know the rules. Develop healthy bedtime rituals. Have a warm bath, but don't overheat the bedroom. Make sure the room is dark and quiet. If necessary unplug the telephone but wear earplugs. Avoid stimulants (coffee, tea) and depressants (booze) before going to sleep. Don't exercise just before sleep. Don't get into the habit of using sleeping pills. Practice meditation if it helps.

Recent evidence suggests that "Napping is good". Various people from Churchill onwards have stressed the power of a good nap. A 20-minute nap can be highly beneficial. So, employers take note. Schedule for naps and have places that facilitate them.

There are duties for successful night shift work employers and employees. The employers provide a well-lit environment with good facilities (microwave oven, fridge, drinks, etc and so on). They schedule shifts with reasonable breaks and days off. They do not encourage overtime. They promote healthy napping and, where they can, help workers get to and from work. They are serious about health and safety rules and regulations.

And successful shift workers? They take short breaks and do some exercise in them. They eat healthily. They keep a diary of drowsiness and don't leave either boring or important tasks to this period. They watch out for their friends and get them to do the same. They learn from how others do or do not cope well with the problems.

So shift work is here to stay. To avoid accidents and lawsuits, absenteeism and poor morale, both employer and employee need to wake up to the fact that they need to plan and practice for working in these biologically unusual circumstances.

Space exploration

It has become fashionable to explain much of human behavior, even at work, in terms of sociobiology. We are indeed *naked apes*, whose apparent sophistication and development is paper thin. So much of what we do is governed by caveman needs and concerns.

Few doubt that we are fiercely territorial animals. Neighbors literally kill each other because of very minor infringements of plants, trees and hedges. And we still laugh at the beach-towels-around-the-pool behavior of our European friends, eager to mark their territorial possession.

Space at work is always a hotbed of contention. Office size is, or was, a pure index of power. The view from your window (if you are lucky enough to have one) may be important too. How close or far from certain facilities (car park, canteen, customers) also make your space less or more desirable.

The size, shape and location of workspace for many people is a result of accident and history. Certain spaces, be they offices, cubicles, or just desks in a room, are usually considered more desirable than others. People have, over time, maneuvered themselves, either with or without official blessing, so that those with most seniority or service get the best space. Strange walls of files, and desks can re-emphasize the distinction between public and private space, between my and your bit, and between good and bad space.

Architects, designers and ergonomists are often appalled by what people do in offices to rearrange their space. They do things that go completely against the original concepts, clear aesthetics and even common sense, let alone health and safety requirements.

Workspace allocation and entitlement really comes to the fore when people move buildings. Take an intact department, even a whole organization with all its psychological complexity and try to relocate it. Struggles for power and superiority begin. Old animosities can surface.

The best predictor of friendship at work is propinquity. You get to like those you see most often. That is why you marry the girl/boy next door. Enemies we put at arm's length. Or, at least, friends become acquaintances become strangers as they drift away spatially as well as psychologically.

So a physical move nearly always leads to a psychological move. Indeed, some managers use a physical move to attempt to achieve corporate culture change. Most often it is to save money and the change can lead to many unforeseen consequences, mostly negative if the move is from closed to open plan. The two central questions for managers are workspace allocation and entitlement. They are closely related and very "hot" problems.

Entitlement can be considered essentially by four options. It can be and usually is select provision of space decided by all sorts of factors: rank, task, history. Your workspace can be a reward for *long service* or *task complexity* or because you did well in the past. Sometimes the criteria for space entitlement are explicit, but frequently not. As anyone who moves house knows, it is profoundly disturbing and surfaces some issues that have "sunk to the bottom of the pool".

Old animosities can arise over space-entitlement debates. People feel challenged on how, when, where and indeed why they work as they do. Things become exposed – all very upsetting. And answers to reasonable and rational questions are wrapped in powerful emotional overtones.

Another entitlement method is *universal provision*. Whoever you are, whatever you do, however long you have labored in this particular vineyard, you will get the same space. And it is more than likely to be open space. Soon one can feel particularly exposed and vulnerable and rendered equal despite patent non-equality in input and output.

This democratic option becomes ever more popular despite massive resistance, special pleading, even attempts at sabotage. But it can be and is often enforced with a sense of ideological zealotry.

There are two other options. One is that space allocation is done by *work teams*. The team gets the space and works out between the team members how it is used. This shifts the problem from the manager to the work leader.

The last option is becoming most common but seems to fly in the face of what we know about our animal past, our basic instincts and needs. This is *non-territorial* allocation. This is not even the world of hot-desking. It is the world of each day finding a space and working there. And it presents the same dilemmas and tactics as the holiday sunbathers who all want to mark their territory around the pool at least a day in advance.

Whatever the management gurus might say and whatever the explicit values of the organization (manifest in the "vision thing"), space-entitlement decisions are often made on criteria that are not strictly democratic, fair, logical or even profit-oriented.

Space can be allocated by grade/level/seniority, by task or function, or simply giving everyone the same. It is easiest to make an argument for doing allocation by task. Given the nature of the task (that is, complexity), or the nature of the tools, people need different space. Complex cognitive tasks might not need much space (except between the ears), but they usually require that people have a quiet (that is, non-shared) space.

Other tasks require frequent team interaction and the space can be designed to facilitate easy work flow.

What you do, when you do it, and how you do it seem reasonable criteria for meeting out the cubic meters. There will, of course, be odd mavericks who claim that they can't work except under particular spatial conditions. This is usually somewhere between special pleading, flim-flam and downright attention-seeking.

For the ergonomist or architect, the task is to understand the nature of the work, optimal conditions and design around them. Unfortunately this may fly in the face of organizational politics, powerful lobbies and of course our animal past. The alpha male will always grab more space whatever he does for a living. There is always more to meeting out the meters than meets the eye!

Specialists and generalists

The tea-boy to managing director story may once have been possible. But the route to the top now always begins with having specialist knowledge and skills while learning how the business works. Over time one acquires broader perspectives, people skills and the "vision thing". Well, some do.

In America it is said most influential, high-profile CEOs started in marketing. In Britain most appear to start life as accountants, even actuaries. Of course, some start out as engineers or lawyers. A few (curiously very few) even start in sales and human resources.

Can and do all specialists become generalists? The answer is clearly "No". Every organization wrestles with the problem of the brilliant specialist most often in a highly numerate area who seems to have neither people skills nor curiosity about the wider world of business.

Goleman, author of the best-selling book on Emotional Intelligence, offers a part exploration. The specialist can often be spotted in early adolescence. They are usually boys, often bright, frequently introverted.

The story goes like this: certain young people find social relations difficult. They have to learn all those adult social skills of persuasion, negotiation, self presentation – in short, "charm". Whilst they may have a few close friends who share common interests, they tend not to be very sociable. And although they may be attracted to having a close relationship (often with the opposite sex), they seem rather confused about what to do, when and why.

Because friendship formation is problematic they tend to withdraw into an interesting, controllable and challenging fantasy world dominated by computers. As a result of years of this activity they become very smart. And this is where the vicious cycle begins. Adolescence is a critical period for learning social skills of getting along with others. They need to understand the origin and consequences of their own and others' emotions. And how to change them. Our "techies" tend not to be comfortable or natural communicators. They don't read people well. They are not very psychologically minded. In short they have low EQ.

But eschewing all the temptations of social life means that these bright introverts have probably done very well in secondary and tertiary education. They often tumble numbers well; are technologically highly sophisticated and excellent analysts. They tend to do well at school and university. And they find that people like them end up in the same class. Indeed lecturers may be struck by the homogeneity of temperament and talent in a final-year engineering, maths or physics class. They are smart, analytic, convergent thinkers rather low on social skills, even with each other.

It is they who often become talented IT people, accountants, actuaries and engineers. It is not unusual to find whole departments of these individuals who have similar talents, outlooks and skills. They select and socialize with each other. And they feel comfortable around others who are like them and who they respect.

The problem arises when they are promoted. Promotion means that supervision, management and leader skills are as, if not more important, than technical skills. And they have to manage support staff who may be rather different from themselves. And they may have to liaise with other departments, customers and share-holders.

As well as things they may do well – data analysis, strategic planning, integrating systems – they are required to do the soft stuff. This includes such things as performance appraisals, attempting to detect and raise morale, dealing with under-performance. In short do the people thing.

Specialists react to these new challenges in many ways. Some try hard to learn them, and some succeed. Some try to find a "deputy" (often a woman) who does the soft stuff: the boss does strategy and is the task leader, the deputy does morale and is the socio-emotional leader.

But the third method is simply to ignore the soft stuff. Communicate dictates by email, be hard to get at. Downplay the HR requirements to set goals, give feedback and the like.

And the result? Neither the specialists enjoy the job, nor the people enjoy being managed by them. They have less time to do what they enjoy and are good at. And they are required to do the things the specialist path never prepared them for.

Promoting brilliant technical specialists into general management roles has many problems. Generally there are three "solutions" to this near intractable problem. The first is to promote managers in title only. They become titular managers carrying on but with money and title. They keep doing what they are good at and enjoy.

The second more risky solution is get in a professional manager without specialist training to do the role. So you may find a professional manager with no accountancy training managing accountants. The theory is that they do not need great depth of knowledge in accountancy to manage well. Maybe? It can as a strategy massively "piss off" the specialists who believe both that their advancement path is being blocked and that you really do need specialist knowledge to really understand the issues and the problems.

The third method is to persevere with clever selection and training. Find those talented specialists who have shown some evidence of people skills. Give them intensive coaching. Reward them for doing the soft stuff well.

They say it takes one psychologist to change a light bulb, but that the psychologist needs to want it to be changed. Equally a specialist can become a good general manager but they need to know really what it entails and to learn to acquire the appropriate skills.

Speeches, sermons and seminar presentations

What is the difference between a well received political speech, a thoughtful sermon and a lucid seminar presentation? The answer is "Very little". They are all about the art of oratory and the rules of rhetoric.

Of course the concept of rhetoric can be used both positively and negatively. A "rhetorical question" is merely for show; "rhetorically inclined" may mean using lofty, pompous or exaggeratedly insincere prose.

But the art of public speaking is a must for any senior executive. This is all about packaging content to become believable, persuasive and memorable. Public speaking can also be a highly lucrative post-successful-career hobby. Washed-up politicians, sportspeople and academics long to be on the after-dinner circuit.

Some people are more natural speakers than others. The extroverted; the articulate; the vocal seem to have an advantage. They have learnt early the power of a good yarn, be it round the campfire, the dinner-party table or the boardroom.

However talented, or indeed talentless, one is, it is possible to acquire skills. The young curate has to master the 10-minute sermon, the aspiring MP the soap-box speech to the crowd and the chairman the annual address to the shareholders' meeting.

A great deal of the effectiveness of any talk lies, of course, in the content. But just as brilliantly structured, witty, even profound content can be spoilt, unappreciated or go unnoticed by poor delivery, so style can sometimes compensate for content.

There are many amusing yet essentially useful mnemonics for the public speaker. Some preachers talk of pace, pause and pitch. Read a sermon you have heard and it can seem thin or rambling. But great preachers know the value of pace: pace changes, slow for profound, fast for excitement or wit.

They know also about both forms of pitch: content pitch and sound pitch. The former means getting the content right for the audience – neither too highfalutin nor patronizing. Equally it is important that the speaker can be heard clearly.

And there is also the very important issue of the pause. Pause for effect, pause for reflection, pause for profundity. Too many politicians have forgotten this. Perhaps in their manic desire to "keep the conch shell" during the

Paxman interview, politicians have forgotten the power of the pause. Pauses can be interpreted as doubt, dysphasia, dither. But they can, and should, be used to great effect.

Business people do not generally think of themselves as orators. They simply want to ensure they "get across" an accessible, high impact, memorable message. They are told to "keep it simple, stupid" and to look confident, comfortable and committed while "doing the speech" even if not written by themselves.

Speech writers however know a thing or two about rhetorical devices. They have ABCs, such as *a*nticipation, *b*alance and *c*omparison. Many have studied the techniques of other great orators. They have deconstructed Churchill, Kennedy and Martin Luther King to find their codes.

And there is a list of useful tips to remember. Contrasts are good: the bad past, the glorious future. Contradiction resolution is good, as are comparing opposites. Us and them, the saved and the damned, the path to prosperity and the road to ruin.

It's good to resolve the problem if it means creating false problems in the first place. And there is a magic number. Somehow lists of three words or ideas have a cadence and a force that two or four do not.

People like stories and anecdotes even if they bear a fairly tenuous relationship to the truth. Ronald Reagan was a memorable exponent of the art. Stories are memorable, easily retold. They can, like parables, have multiple meanings.

But good speech writers have to understand the craft of the poet. This is the art of exploiting and exploring not only the meaning but the sound of words and the pictures conjured up by analogies, similes and metaphors.

So the lessons? Tell them what you are going to tell them; tell them; tell them what you have told them. Tweak their emotions by appealing to their deepest values and anxieties. Make them believe in you by heroic visions of a new and better world. Remember the power of the story, phrase or anecdote which becomes the slogan.

Throw away Power Point and creative artists. Learn the art of the scriptwriter, read poetry and great speeches. And practice, practice, practice.

Striking a balance

Various civil servant groups periodically go on strike. When politicians get applause for the idea of cutting civil servant jobs it often leads to strikes, stoppages, work-to-rule or other forms of protest.

But how effective is the strike? What are the alternatives? Can disagreements be resolved more amicably for all concerned especially the long suffering public whose servants won't serve?

Everything about the concept of the strike seems so dated. One thinks about the General Strike of 1926 and the Miners strike in the early 1980s. The images of people walking behind great nineteenth-century banners seems an icon of a distant past: of an industrial, manufacturing country with labor and capital locked in eternal dispute.

Some of the residue of strikes remains in the quaint and totally inappropriate terminology: civil servants "take industrial action". Voltaire said the Holy Roman Empire was neither holy, nor Roman, nor Empire. So civil servants are not in the industrial sector nor do they take action. Indeed, they stop it.

The modern strike may be as much about publicity as it is about resolving conflicts. Clever strikers understand photo opportunities, soundbites, attractive and articulate spokespeople. They know that half the battle is winning public sympathy – and that is not easy when they know "slashing bureaucracy and waste in the public sector" is a sure vote winner.

Strikes can backfire: lack of public support can stiffen government resolve and even encourage them to look for more opportunities to "introduce efficiency". Further, cynics love to point out that when certain groups go on strike nobody notices so implying that the jobs are pointless in the first place.

Strikes can do all sorts of unintended damage. They can reduce morale further by causing conflict between those who do and those who do not strike: traditionally the distinction between "scabs" and "non-scabs".

And there are hidden costs. Think of what a one-day strike means for those in Payroll (assuming they too are not on strike). First someone has to determine who actually was or was not on strike. How is this done? By self-report, by observation, by report of others (spies of one sort or another). Then a day's pay (or whatever) has to be calculated and removed from some people and not others. All the more difficult if there are wild-cat, irregular strikes. This can be so problematic some management simply brush the issue under the carpet, and strikers know it.

But there are some advantages to striking. It certainly raises the public profile of the strikers. In recent years civil servants have become increasingly invisible to the public, especially as jobs seem increasingly performed by computers. The clerk who wrote your giro by hand was long ago replaced by a computer paying money into your account. Together with outsourcing and privatization, many would be hard pressed to name more than a few, usually large, civil service departments. Strike action lets people know you are there and, by inconveniencing your customers, that your job is significant.

Old-fashioned, pointless, self-defeating and hurtful only to those (sometimes vulnerable) people that one is trained to serve? Perhaps, but what are the alternatives? Assume that one is a hard-working, trained and educated civil servant who has, according to all records, had an exemplary career. Promises have been made, expectations created and suddenly you are told you are to be either (a) made redundant, (b) relocated to just outside Hull, (c) compulsorily retrained, or (d) retrained in Hull.

The theory says that one undergoes a sequential series of emotions: surprise, shock, feelings of helplessness, depression, anger and then perhaps acceptance. One can go from disbelief to fury in a fairly short amount of time. And this may explain why otherwise mild-mannered, middle-aged professionals take to the street disinhibited in their rage.

The alternatives to many seem few and pointless. One could of course "go to arbitration", though that could be a very long and protracted business. There is the awful "work to rule" alternative for the obstinate obsessives. Some may even rejoice in the opportunity to "go early" so as to retire to one's garden or indeed start a new career.

Uncivil servants beware! Striking in today's economic climate may indeed draw attention to their employment conditions, but seriously antagonize the various publics they are supposed to serve.

The task and the process

Consultants, psychologists and trainers are guilty of spreading various management myths. Perhaps that it is too strong. Suffice to say they may have placed emphasis on the wrong things too often.

This is nowhere more apparent than in the talk about teams. Trainers rush you into the great outdoors to cross ravines, paddle lakes and walk burning coals to demonstrate your interdependence on others, and your courage. Psychologists urge you to complete questionnaires that examine your team-role preferences to help you find the ideal team and your place in it.

Consultants look at health of teams and burble on with amusing stage-wise theories supposing that teams form, norm, storm, perform and adjourn. They may be obsessed with team dynamics particularly if they are pathologically dysfunctional. All the more important if the team is *the* management board.

The major objection to the emphasis on team roles and psychological processes is that they miss out on the most obvious and fundamental point that teams are brought together very specifically to do a task.

Tasks that involve team work have certain characteristics. There are many examples of these teams in action: an airplane flight crew is a team; so are those in a hospital operating theatre. Celebrity cooks have a team in the kitchen and the board of a big organization is a team. Each member of the team has a different skill but similar aims and objectives.

Teams are thus heterogeneous and homogeneous at the same time. Nearly all real effective teams have the concept of specialization of labor. In many ways they are collections of experts whose knowledge, skills and experience add something to the group. Working together means they get to know how, why and what others do but they stick to their bit. So in the operating theatre the surgeon, the anaesthetist and the theatre matron know their role.

Inevitably, however, teams are fairly heterogeneous because different types are attracted to different training and jobs. At board meetings the quiet, detail-oriented CEO might appear very different from the ebullient, big-picture, blue-sky marketing Director. They may have different personalities but share similar aims and thus values.

All teams struggle with the entropy that seems to "tug" them towards homogeneity. It's always easier being around people like oneself: people with the same language, values and upbringing. But also people with the same personality and thinking style, the same energy and passions, the same hopes and fears.

Yet it is precisely because people in teams have different skills and abilities that they are likely to have differences. Somebody has to be a good spokesperson. Somebody needs to understand legal documents. Somebody needs to bring alignment and harmony in times of strife. Extroverts prefer certain tasks, introverts others. But they need to get on.

Functional, successful teams have frequent contact. Their interactions are inevitably both task and non-task oriented. That is, they get on with it, but also "shoot the breeze". And in doing so they get to understand each other better and hopefully like and respect each other more.

And at the heart of the matter is respect. Healthy teams respect each other's expertize, contribution, dedication. They understand boundaries both of a social and technical nature.

So beware of loose groups of individuals in parallel with weak relationships. They may do "team talk" but are unlikely to be a team.

And worse, fascination with, and concentration on interpersonal roles and processes approaches the problem from the wrong end. So what if you are a natural resource investigator or a complete finisher? Does it matter if you prefer to be a chairperson or a plant? The task dictates what you need to do and how.

In many teams you may not need creative types, or negotiators. Some are self-managed with a very democratic structure.

The bottom line is this. Successful teams focus on task not process. They optimize their heterogeneity, having different skills and clear boundaries but similar aims. A good team has regular enjoyable social contact and a pervasive spirit of respect for each other's contribution.

Telephone tell-tales

Most selectors use the infamous trio in their business: application form, references and interviews. References are still used but with much more careful examination through fear of litigation.

Indeed, because some people with glowing references have been selected and proven utter disasters, the reference writers and their organizations have been subject to libelous action. Some referees have been instructed simply to specify only the dates an employee worked for an organization and not to give any details about their work performance.

Some recruiters have decided they get better value out of references by asking specific questions about time-keeping, absenteeism and ability, rather than let the referee write anything they want to about the individual.

But more recently selectors are taking a feather from the cap of their more adventurous colleagues, the head-hunters. Rather than provide a written reference, referees are telephoned and asked about the candidate. This has three crucial advantages: it is convenient for the selector/recruiter which means many more references can be obtained; it is easy and quick for the referee; and, most importantly, a conversation where the employer is put on the spot is likely to be more truthful.

That is, the skillful questioner, with assurances of anonymity and/or confidentiality, may well get at the truth about the individual. They may uncover oddities, idiosyncrasies and inadequacies they never could in a traditional written reference.

Most important in all this is what is called the 360-degree, or the multi-rater, aspect. The traditional reference is predominantly "downward". The referee has been the teacher, manager, supervisor or in some other sense superior of the employee. Thus, the ingratiator or those skillful in "managing up" may get glowing references, while those not in the "apple-polishing business" don't fare as well.

But what is it like to work for, that is, be managed by, this individual? What is their management style? To what extent are they perfectionist, obsessional, impulsive or error-prone? Can and do they motivate and delegate? Do they show favoritism? How do they cope with stress?

And what about their peers or those people at the same age, stage and level? Although peers may be competitors, they often have a good sense of a person's ability. Studies have shown that "peer ratings" of ability, motivation and style are amongst the most predictive of all methods. You know your peers, share with them hopes, worries, foibles, insights and the like. Most people confide in them much more than they do in superiors or subordinates.

The boss knows the consequences or products of an individual's work; the peers their abilities and motives; and their subordinates their work style. It is only by interviewing *all* of them that a real picture of the individual can be built up.

The telephone-reference technique can be used to test hypotheses. It can yield interesting data as well. What if an individual is seen quite differently by different groups? A person might be passionately loved and hated, admired and despised at the same time. This probably indicates a strong, possibly idiosyncratic style which suits some very well but not others.

The Freudians maintain that people cannot, rather than will not, always tell you about their motives and what really drives them at work. We are all energized by power, influence, fame and money. But our motivational profile is often pretty unique and obscured to ourselves, partly for protection. But shrewd observers of our work-related behavior see patterns and themes that enable then to deduce what really drives us.

So get on the blower. Forget written references and expensive 360-degree questionnaires. Plan some simple, high-yield and discriminating questions for those that really know the person you are interested in.

Titular realities

Imagine you saw a job offer that tickled your fancy. It was "right up your street". Nice package, ideal location, matches your work experience perfectly.

But what is the job title? Does is matter if everything else is OK? Would it seriously affect your applying? Consider the following baker's dozen job titles in alphabetical order: Administrator, Adviser, Business Partner, Coach, Counselor, Consultant, Director, Facilitator, Head, Lead, Manager, Officer, Team Leader. Of course, if you are an American the whole puzzle has been happily solved. All are Executive Vice Presidents. All chiefs, no Indians. But this, fortunately, is England.

Does it really matter what you are called? What determines an organization's choice of title terminology? Does it have PR or HR or IR consequences?

Administrator sounds dull, bureaucratic, passive. It's hard to think of administrators as sexy, or dynamic, or proactive. *Adviser* is more disinterested, more consultant-like. You go to advisers only in need: they are not central to the exercise. And don't only ditherers need advice? Hardly a core-sounding job.

Business Partner sounds OK, but a trifle ambiguous. Why are you partnering rather than running? Is your job to inject business reality to those less concerned about it? Clearly a term useful only in specific circumstances.

And *Coach*? Some organizations have internal coaches, not expensively paid managerial fashion accessories who try a couple of hours of therapy once a month. The aim perhaps is to suggest it is the (primary) job of the manager to teach, enthuse, inspire and motivate their staff.

Counselor is quite posh. Senior diplomats are called Counselors. But this is far too easily confused with the non-directive, tea-and-sympathy person who listens to your woes. Hardly the image for a thrusting, successful, dynamic business.

Consultant? Enough said: a simple organism designed to translate bullshit into air miles. Failed middle managers put out to grass and trying to redevelop themselves. Too many of them. Too loaded a term.

Director is the business: on the board; amongst the grown-ups; the top table. Directors tell others what to do. Grander than manager and, therefore, surely the most attractive of the job titles available.

Facilitator sounds too non-job, temporary. Focus groups and training courses are facilitated by extroverted, uninhibited types whose sole purpose seems to be to get you "going" on some issue. Hardly the job for a serious grown-up.

Head is OK. It says you are the boss. The buck stops with you. *Lead* is slightly different – not as common, but clearly the one in charge. But at what level?

Manager is the most common term. So common, in fact, that most organizations distinguish between junior, middle and senior managers. Some organizations have as many as 80% of the staff with the term manager in their title. From "Assistant Manager" to "Manager's Assistant" and from the perplexing "Manager of Special Projects" to "Executive Manager". Boring and ever more confusing. Surely one could do better.

Surprisingly many non-military organizations use the term *Officer*. It is not clear if they are commissioned or uncommissioned, field-rank or not. There are officers and men. Above and below the salt. Those who command and those who obey. Bit stuffy; bit old-fashioned; bit public-sector for some. *Team Leader* is very unmilitary. First among equals, egalitarian, democratic, consultative.

So whence the choice? The history of the organization perhaps. Thus just as "staff department" became "personnel", became "human relations", became "people department," so an "officer" became an "administrator", became a "manager" became a "coach". History, restructuring, the use of consultants, maverick CEOs, and even the PR machine may have an input into how jobs are titled.

But they do make a difference. They affect how people see themselves. They influence others' expectations of what people do and how they do it. In many ways they reflect values just as much as mission statements and "vision thingies".

So next time the organization restructures and "rattles your cage" think of the messages that are sent *and* received when new job titles arise and old ones are quietly forgotten. It is much more important than you may think.

Trust at work

All the figures point in the same direction. Public trust in public institutions is on the decline. It is as steady as it is dramatic. Nearly all the great cherished institutions of yesteryear are now held in much less esteem: the church, the courts, the monarchy.

And those at the bottom of the scale have fallen even further, if indeed that is possible. Politicians rank with estate agents and used-car salesmen. And they are worried. People vote less, respect authority less, feel more alienated. So what to do about it?

The argument is about replacing the "S" words with the "T" words. The former are secrecy, self-interest, spin, suppression and the latter transparency, trust and truth. The solution, it seems, is openness. If the public can see how the great public institutions operate, they will come to respect (and trust) them again.

So far, however, it seems the more organizations talk about openness, the less they are trusted. Ironic, paradoxical even, but there it is. Indeed the very transparency of organizational practice may just be precisely the factor that leads to mis- and distrust.

There are complex issues with the concepts of transparency. Should all public organizations be equally transparent? What of MI5 or MI6? Or the Police and the Armed Forces? And what should be transparent, in product (*What* decisions are made) or process (*How* decisions are made)? Both? Neither? It depends.

And should the organization be proactive or reactive? Should they answer questions when we ask them or tell us all the time?

Will the Freedom of Information Act reduce or increase paranoia? Is it a charter for obsessional, conspiracy theorists and the paranoid? Or will it herald a new era of open governments, involvement and participation?

The Scandinavian countries are usually held up as models of trust, transparency and good government. They used also to be held up as models of real socialism until it proved unworkably costly.

But they do seem to enjoy open government, bicycling royals and transparency. They are also deeply regulated and taxed societies, where things seem to be either banned or compulsory.

The question is whether respect for and trust in authority is simply a function of transparency and openness. Perhaps it's a cultural value. It is also a property of individuals.

A famous neo-psychoanalyst Eric Ericson pointed out that one of the earliest and most important stages of psychosocial development is the development of trust. He argued that when a mother's care is sensitive, confident and consistent, the child is more likely to develop a basic trust of others and self, and a sense of confidence when an adult. This child will see the world as safe and supportive and a place where one can rely on others. The unlucky child, however, never learns to trust others and may be plagued throughout life with feelings of anxiety and estrangement.

Some people are more trusting than others. Children are trusting and learn to be less so. Trusting sounds naive. You also trust in the Almighty – often when there is no hope left. To be skeptical and wary seems wise.

Some adults take things on trust, but others do not. This may be a generalized trait, or something restricted to various facets of life. So you might trust your Church, but not your Council. You may trust your Doctor but not your Dentist.

People tend to trust or mistrust individuals, rather than organizations, though there is, of course, generalization from one to the other. So your trust in the health service is essentially a function of how you are usually treated at your local surgery or clinic.

Similarly, trust in the police is often a function of very direct experience of dealing with theft and robbery and, more likely these days, traffic offenses.

The question is this. Can one try to turn around trust in public services? In the great institutions of the state and in our elected (and hereditary) leaders, through a policy of more openness and transparency? Perhaps – but was it lost through lack of transparency, or is this a shift in the zeitgeist to a more savvy, individualistic, more rights-than-responsibilities society?

Indeed, where have examples of organizations becoming more open led to an increase in trust? It did not work with the monarchy.

There is a difference between privacy and secrecy, between discretion and dishonesty, policy and paranoia, and speaking-out and spin.

Uncertainty avoidance

After the war, a group of American and German social scientists attempted to understand the "Mind of the Nazis". They interviewed many of the major perpetrators, including Goering before he killed himself, to try to get an insight into "how they ticked".

The result of their effort was a book called *The Authoritarian Personality*, which looked at the personality traits and processes associated with what might euphemistically be called "interpersonal intolerance". One trait that they identified was called *intolerance of ambiguity*. It is now called uncertainty avoidance or, more colloquially, "managing the grey". This has been identified as an important interpersonal, corporate and cultural difference factor in business life.

All of us would like to be sure we lived in a stable, predictable, just, and certain world. Randomness, chaos and capriciousness are truly terrifying and we all invest a lot of energy trying to combat these forces of darkness. But our need for clarity, certainty and decisiveness differs from individual to individual and country to country.

In Britain, we have no written constitution. In the law we muddle along on a case-by-case basis eschewing any grand Code Napoleon. We positively revel in subtle meaningless differences like "The Bishop of England" (York) versus "The Bishop of All England" (Canterbury).

Uncertainty avoidance can be considered at the national, the organizational and the individual differences level. The British can, it appears, cope with uncertainty. We are like the Indians and the Swedes and the Danes. But research indicates that other countries are rather different in this respect. The Belgians and Japanese, the Greeks and the Portuguese have a stronger need to avoid uncertainty.

There are, it appears, all sorts of differences between low (us) and high uncertainty-avoidance cultures. Compared to those which score highly on uncertainty avoidance, cultures with lower scores are more accepting of dissent, more tolerant of deviance, more positive to the young, less risk averse, less happy about showing emotion.

But organizations and industries can also be categorized on this dimension. Indeed it is likely that the intolerant or uncertainty-avoiding seek out (and even seek to change) organizations that "fit" with their own preferences. Again, researchers who have contrasted low and high uncertainty-avoiding organizations see clear differences. The more tolerant tend to have less stress, live more in the present than the future, show less emotional resistance to change and tend to have more highly achievement-motivated people. Tolerant companies tend to be smaller, with a smaller generation gap and a lower average age for higher-level jobs. The ethos is that managers should be selected on ability rather than seniority, that managers need not be an expert in the field they manage and that generalists are preferable over specialists.

Organizations that do not have a problem with ambiguity and uncertainty seem to favor broad guidelines over clear requirements and instructions; they believe rules may be broken for pragmatic reasons and have no problem with conflict and competitiveness. More tolerant managers are more happy to delegate, compromise and deal with "foreigners" or people from other ethnic groups.

But it is not all good news for low uncertainty-avoidance organizations. They tend to have higher labor turnover and the job-satisfaction scores of people in them are lower. Managers report and indeed have less power. But they are much less bureaucratic.

Managers who have problems with uncertainty avoidance are afraid of, and made deeply uncomfortable by uncertainty and ambiguity. People think of them as straightforward and predictable though not creative. There are certainly areas of work where they will thrive, like health and safety, production, but others where they would be deeply uncomfortable, like advertising or R&D.

Understanding understatement

We have been called perfidious Albion: treacherous. But whence this treachery? Surely it is simply a matter of misunderstanding. It is not as if we say one thing and do another. Foreigners simply don't understand what we are saying. They are so literal.

In England the loudest cheer in sports competitions is for the person who comes last, not first. We love our maverick failures like 'Eddy-the-Eagle Edwards', whose abject failure at the Olympic ski jump made him our favorite and a national hero. We celebrate Dunkirk, the result of a massive military defeat. We admire Captain Scott, who was beaten to the Pole by Amundsen.

We are, it seems, neither American nor European in our use of understatement. We are therefore often misunderstood by those who see us as either pathetically low in self-esteem or desperately inadequate. To the ears of many brought up on the self-esteem movement, we may even seem chronically depressed, urgently in need of therapy.

The English enjoy and are often brought up on the virtues of *self-deprecation*. Being *self-effacing* is encouraged. *Humility* is far better than hubris. *Restraint* is more adult than enthusiasm. *Detachment* is a sign of strength. Better to deny than exaggerate ability. Better to be inconspicuous than bask in the limelight.

No other nation does it as well. Few other people understand it. But in what sense is understatement functional or beneficial?

First, a true story. Late in the day a worker is seen wandering down the corridor, squash racket and associated togs in hand, on his way to play on the company court. A visiting American spots him and says "Ah, I see that you play squash. So do I. How good are you?" On the surface this is a perfectly reasonable question. It is no fun whatsoever for people of quite different standards to play each other.

But how do you respond? If you play at a serious level, the "correct" response is probably "Not too bad". Everyone knows that "not too bad" is a useful phrase to describe everything from zero ability to state of health. It means essentially "excellent", "robust", in fact "very good".

From here responses descend via "so-so" to "pretty awful" to "totally hopeless". Last of all is the response that one simply does not do it. Thus, if one's French or German is good enough for idle chatter and day-to-day interaction, but not for higher level negotiations or sophisticated dinner parties, one may even disclaim any knowledge of that language.

The squash racket carrying Englishman was top of the company squash ladder, an Oxbridge blue and a county player and "not too bad". The American shrugged and indicated that that was a pity because he himself was a rather talented player.

A trivial misunderstanding. There have been examples in war when British and American commanders have really misunderstood each other. "Things are getting a bit sticky" or "slight problem here" can sound to the American ear not very serious, where the British may understand "very serious indeed".

Whence this self-deprecation, understatement, undue modesty? The opposite of course is arrogance, exaggeration, personal trumpet-blowing. Arrogance, hubris, self-importance are seen as unfair, unattractive and unwise. Unfair because although we know ability and talent are normally distributed, it is quite inappropriate to show off your God-given (or even personally earned) talents. People are even tempted to attribute their success to good fortune rather than ability. Unattractive because boastfulness, pride and hubris are not only sinful but impolite. They make those less talented feel worse about themselves.

But most important of all, hubris is unwise. Arrogance attracts enemies and it leads to envy. How the mighty can fall. How tempting it is to puncture the massively inflated balloon of the hubris-filled pompous fool. Many a politician has paid dearly for this error.

On the other hand, self-deprecation reduces threat. It may even attract sympathy. The less able seem quite happy to treat you as one of theirs. If you don't blow your own trumpet others will do it for you. And, paradoxically, honors are more likely to be heaped upon you.

The British, perhaps intuitively, know that self-esteem is the consequence, not the cause, of success. But are the self-deprecating, self-effacing, understating British a dying breed? Are they the stuff of black-and-white movies? The war generation? Did they ever exist in the first place, or are they merely a figment of movie-directors' imagination?

Certainly, not all British "did" humility. It may be caught in time and limited to certain social classes. Understatement may be under attack by the self-esteem movement that sees self-deprecation as tantamount to mental illness.

The secret, of course, lies in knowing one's real ability but not boasting about it. Self-deprecation is done from a position of strength, not weakness. It is not aimed to deceive but to help social intercourse. And it will continue to be a source of bafflement to foreigners.

Why would anyone want to work for you?

For the naive, inexperienced selector there are now self-help books available on "clever clogs" questions to ask at interview. People buy them both to impress fellow interviewers, perhaps the major point of the whole exercise, and to try and fox the interviewee.

Others have favorite personal questions that they have honed over the years. They may be the result of personal experience and theories, half-digested Freudian ideas or copying someone else. And these "killer" questions can range from the bizarre to the quirky: "Given I know you well and am being honest, what is your favorite compliment?"

The trouble with this technique is that it is not clear what the answers mean. Often the interviewer simply likes to see the interviewees squirm as they try to reconcile disparate issues like political correctness, dissimulation requirements and purported company values. There are good answers, clever answers, evasive answers, diplomatic answers, but do they help in selection?

The interest in 360-degree feedback has alerted people to three facts. First, people at work live in a world that is surprisingly free from feedback, yet receiving accurate and sensitive feedback can be a salutary and useful learning experience. Secondly, different people have very different opinions about an individual's management ability depending on the data they have on them and the style in which they like to be managed. Thirdly, observers (that is boss, peers and subordinates) tend to agree more often with one another than the individual's own evaluation.

From this work, some consultants have suggested that all managers end an appraisal or progress review with the simple but discriminating question "How do you experience my management style?" "Style" is a good word because it suggests both choice and change. If it isn't working or not appreciated, one simply changes it to something more appropriate.

But there is an excellent question to ask an applicant: "Why would anyone want to work for you?" It is a sort of upward selection question. That is, while most selection decisions are downward because senior people choose those who will work for, or study under them, it is possible to have the reverse.

People are asked to choose, nominate or vote for their boss. In a sense this is what politics is about: voting for people who in fact rule us. Politicians talk about their policies although some unwisely talk about their principles or traits.

The question asks a candidate to explain, why they, in the eyes of their prospective team (subordinate) might be the best (most suitable or desirable) candidate. It is question that can tickle both hubris and humility.

What would a wise candidate say? Would he or she peddle out inane platitudes about their history of success in the past, their education, their warmth?

Clever, or at least well-read, candidates would know that there is an important extant literature on this topic. What it shows is that if you give people a list of all desirable traits in a boss: caring, supportive, loyal, mature, and so on, they always choose one trait above all the others – integrity. They also want their managers to be able (bright, competent, intelligent) and motivational (forward-looking, inspiring). Other factors, even courageous, dependable, determined or self-controlled come way behind.

What does it mean? It suggests people prefer to be managed by those who tell the truth, unpalatable though it may be. They prefer this to spin, flim flam or silence. That is why the BBC and Churchill were so admired during the war. You got the bad news straight, and with a strong message of resolve. But integrity goes further. It means adhering to the law, not going back on one's word and so on.

It is more self-evident why people want bright and inspiring bosses. Intelligence is indeed the best predictor of success at work. Bright bosses learn faster, adapt more easily, solve problems more efficiently. And who does not want a boss able to inspire? Someone who can rally the troops, stiffen the sinews, squeeze that drop of extra effort out of the team to accomplish the goals.

So why would anyone want to work for you? Well sir, I believe my record shows a history of honesty in all my dealings, real competence in my skills and an ability to inspire others. That should clinch it.

Workplace spirituality

One hundred years ago a German polymath called Weber wrote a treatise that is debated to this day. He proposed that religious beliefs endorsed and fed the spirit of capitalism. Salvation comes through work. All work is for God's glory. And wealth, one consequence of hard work, is a sign of God's grace. The rich are the chosen, the poor the damned.

The idea of the work ethic has been debated ever since. A wide variety of issues, from a rise in delinquency and illiteracy to a decrease in productivity and commitment, have been blamed on the demise of the fundamental tenets of the work ethic.

Some argue the work ethic has not gone away. Rather it has simply been transformed. Time management, DIY and health-scare asceticism are all part of the new work ethic. Further, sport has been protestantized with all the emphasis on competition, commitment, and discipline. No pain, no gain – the very core of Puritan beliefs.

And now from America, as always, we see winds of a new fad; workplace spirituality. For some, this idea is about as oxymoronic as "business ethics" or "military intelligence". But is this a rediscovery of the Weberian idea of the connection between religious beliefs and economic output? Conspiracy theorists are quick to see connections between manipulative managers and gullible laborers, particularly in America.

There are now papers, books, handbooks on workplace spirituality. Once you get a handbook you know the field is beginning to mature. But is a 500-page scholarly handbook a milestone, a millstone or a tombstone?

Part of the idea of workplace spirituality originates in the ever popular but evidence-free world of multiple intelligence. One of these is supposedly spiritual intelligence which includes such things as the capacity for transcendence: an ability to invest everyday activities, events and relationships with a sense of the sacred and divine and an ability to "utilize spiritual resonance" (huh?) to solve problems in everyday living. So what is this new fad, supposedly associated with organizational productivity?

A cursory "surfing of the web" indicated a proliferation of websites, newsletters, and conferences all on the topic. However, it is very apparent that the concept has multiple meanings. These include: acting with honesty and integrity in all aspects of work; treating employees, suppliers, shareholders, and customers in a responsible, caring way; having social, environmental, and ecological responsibility by serving the "wider social community"; holding religious study groups and/or prayer/meditation meetings at work; and being able to discuss values without the dogmatism and overstructuring of organized religion.

Certainly there is a range of values that seems to fall under the umbrella of spirituality: accountability, caring, cooperativeness, honesty, integrity, justice, respect, service, and trustworthiness. Spirituality is a means, not an end. It supposedly encourages questions like: Are our business decisions based exclusively on profit? Are employees required to sacrifice private/family time to be successful? Are we self-centered and forgetting the principles of service to others in the wider community? But also, do employees get a sense of wonder at work? Do they have a sense of community?

Another theme rediscovered within the rubric of workplace spirituality is the concept of vocation: to work consciously and to celebrate all aspects of work's purpose. Indeed the word "vocation" has always had both secular and spiritual significance: it can mean both a divine call to religious life and the work in which a person is regularly employed. It implies that the fit is right between person and organization, that they suit each other in terms of preferences, values, and lifestyles.

Skeptics and cynics of the workplace-spirituality concept have such concerns as the imposition of religious concepts or ethics of a particular religious group on everyone. Others are concerned by the superficiality and trivialization of religious and spiritual belief. Some are worried about cost, time-wasting and the potential harassment of the "nonspiritual". It has been suggested that the movement is in fact led by the baby-boomer generation who is now post-materialist and much more aware of its mortality. But it does seem to have "struck a nerve", at least in America.

A focus on workplace spirituality makes the workplace somewhere to express and fulfill one's deeper purpose. Work is an integral part of life and one does not disengage heart or brain at the factory door or office. There is no compensation in work–life balance: both can (perhaps should) be deeply spiritual. People bring to work their attitudes, beliefs, and values about both material and spiritual affairs. Even within more formal religious beliefs historically there has not been a clear distinction between work and non-work. One does not suspend faith and values on entering the workplace. Personal ethics and values are relevant in nearly all aspects of work: from the very choice of vocation itself to the treatment of colleagues and customers.

Conclusion

Managerial Manifestos, Mantras and Mission Statements

Manifesto:	*Public declaration of intentions, motives or views.*
Mantra:	*Sacred word or sound used as an invocation or incantation.*
Mission:	*Ministry commissioned to propagate its faith or carry on humanitarian work.*

Manifestos

Over the years most political parties have radically changed their manifestos. As such they have forsaken ideology for pragmatism. They "listen" to what people want and what troubles them and promise to deliver all/most/ some of those needs. The rhetoric of the grand "isms", like capitalism, socialism, communism, even Thatcherism seems to have been dropped in favor of some more simple exhortations.

So much for party manifestos. What would a good, simple, honest, management manifesto look like? Imagine one had to choose between various, relatively equal jobs. They had similar pay and conditions, but each had slightly different management manifestos. Assuming, and that might be simply naive, that they honored their manifestos and that there was a close relationship between the rhetoric and reality, which would you choose?

Perhaps it would make an excellent assessment-center exercise to ask potential managers to bullet point (and even explain) a few manifesto items. Consider the following. Are they too radical to actually try to live up to? Are they too vague? Do they actually affect shareholder value? What is not there that should be? And vice versa?

1. *We will honor our promises.*
   If and when we make explicit (and possibly even solemn) promises about what we will do, they will be honored (to the best of our ability). This means a promise is an obligation; statement of a real intention. Not just PR flim flam to make you feel better. So they will probably be made less often, and very thoughtfully considered first.

2. *We will model what we want.*
   We will model honestly, time-keeping, conscientiousness, lack of greed, customer-attentiveness, and so on. That is, there will not be a

yawning gap between the things we demand/request of others and how we, ourselves, behave. We too are mortal, fallible and tempted but we will endeavor to ask no more of others than of ourselves.

3.   *We will admit failure.*
There is, inevitably, a lot of failure in business life. Experimentation, innovation and exploration frequently leads to setbacks and failure. The risk-averse never try new things and rarely reach the top. The risk-addicted fail to weigh the balance well and make good judgements. But rather than try to cover up, explain away or downplay failure we will admit it and try to learn lessons from the experience.

4.   *We will endeavor to keep up to date (without being faddist).*
Most organizations strive to be trend-setters rather than trend-followers. They would prefer to be thought of as creative, innovative and ground-breaking rather than solid, sensible and sure. The world is changing fast, certainly with respect to technology. Those organizations full of technophiles are, paradoxically, very behind in people management, just as those in technophobe organizations are slow to embrace, change or ever fully utilize technology.

5.   *We will confront poor performers.*
Most organizations are handicapped by "quit but stay", angry and alienated, half-power workers who do not carry their weight. It takes firmness and courage and a sensible performance management system to confront poor performers early on. This is the "shape up or ship out" message often delivered too meekly, too late and too inconsequentially. The monetary and moral cost of not dealing with chronic poor performance is too high for any organization.

6.   *We will reward effort and ability.*
There are many ways to achieve success but few occur without a combination of effort and ability. We will endeavor to select able people and have policies and procedure to encourage maximum effort. It is the combination of effort and ability that leads to success – one without the other is insufficient. Hence it is important to seek out and nurture ability while simultaneously encouraging maximum effort.

7.   *We will spell out contracts and expect reciprocation.*
It is said people have two contracts at work: the legal and the psychological contracts. Whilst the former is an explicit legal document spelling out agreed obligations, the latter is implicit and about feelings and

expectations. Managers need to make the implicit explicit. They need to discuss mutual expectations of each other on regular occasions. Unless this is done contracts can be broken without the other side knowing the cause or consequences.

8. *We will resist nepotism and favoritism.*
   Every manager seeks to appoint and promote those best suited to the job. Experience, skills and motivation seem critical. Yes, it is often tempting to give additional help or assistance to those who may be related to one, or who one particularly likes. Nepotism and favoritism destroy a sense of fair play, competition and desire to work hard for rewards.

9. *We will spend our money wisely (as if it were our own).*
   We will not carry out a tax-and-spend, bread-and-circuses policy of using stores of cash for foolhardy, rash ideas. There is a difference between cautious and wise, between mean and frugal, and between impulsive and sensible. It is easier to spend others' money. But as share/stake-holders we believe we are spending our own money on plant, advertising, training, and so on. And we believe we will always think clearly and do rational cost–benefit analyses.

10. *We work for our shareholders.*
    We acknowledge that we are in business to make money for our shareholders. Our aim is to create a successful, profitable organization that remains in business. We do so by giving customers what they want; choosing and managing well; investing wisely. Our aim is to stay in business and be economically successful.

The moral of the story is thus. Dispense with repetitive mantras or misleading mission statements. Set out a clear honest management manifesto and stick by it.

Mantras

And what of management mantras? Some individual and organizations appear to believe that the more they repeat a word or phrase the more it will come into being. Keep saying *quality* product, having *quality* circles and somehow, miraculously, you get it. Say people are your most important asset; win an investor in people prize and "hey presto" you have loyal, conscientious, dedicated staff.

Just as there often occurs a decoupling of the mind and mouth when alcohol has flowed, so mantra-management encourages a decoupling between bravado and reality. The PR and the practice of management may be poles apart and this can lead to serious staff cynicism. And cynicism can easily breed disloyalty which, through anything from sabotage to whistle-blowing, can lead to disaster.

Managers need to model behavior rather than chanting popular guru-inspired mantras. In his witty *Cynic's Guide to Management*, McKibbin (1998) lists 25 management styles, all incompetent and all familiar. The styles are extremely funny because they capture the bizarreness of both extraordinary people and organizations. They are brief summaries of his types:

- *Abdication Management:* Abdicating responsibility by calling in others (nearly always management consultants). This is most often done when decisions are difficult or involve personal pain. The strategy is extremely expensive but has the advantage that, if the whole thing fails, the consultant can be blamed.

- *Alibi Management:* Obtaining, refining and rehearsing a long list of alibis as to why service fails. They may be human (staff shortages, sickness), mechanical (an incident at Swindon), electrical (signaling problems), vague (the incoming flight arrived late) or "acts of God" (the weather).

- *Ballcock Management:* A lavatorial analogy where managers contribute precious little to organizational success, being kept afloat by the hard work of others until a cut-off point is reached beyond which they cease to rise. This occurs either when subordinates/peers get "fed up" carrying the ballcock manager or seeing them take credit for what they quite clearly have not done.

- *Beehive Management:* This style dictates that managers emulate the drones in beehives. Occasionally beehive organizations have more than one corpulent "queen" and extensive elaborate dances occur (meetings, lunches) to decide on winners. Sometimes drones can outnumber workers which, of course, is a recipe for disaster.

- *Convoy Management:* This is where management proceeds at the pace of the "slowest-witted" manager. Convoy management rejoices in the rule of "precedent" – doing things in the way in which they have always been done. Fear of innovation and procrastination are the marks of convoy management.

■ *Crisis Management:* This is not the management and resolution of crises but their creation. Crisis managers are the "Typhus Marys" of stress. They are able to conjure up a crisis out of nothing. All setbacks or misfortunes are escalated into crisis. They become masters of hyperbole when discussing day-to-day business.

■ *Cuckoo Management:* Cuckoo managers offer help to close colleagues to overcome problems; most short-term targets take the longer view, then evict them from their own department. Cuckoo managers reap the benefit of watching the competent manager's carefully laid eggs hatch. Cuckoos love mergers and restructuring because it is an ideal time to discover a better nest.

■ *Defensive Management:* Defensive managers try to protect themselves from poor decisions by negating responsibility. Committees, panels and others are constructed with the prime purpose of taking the flak and blame if anything goes wrong.

■ *Displacement Management:* The idea of this style is to displace energies and focus from what you should be doing into more sexy and enjoyable activities that are easier than really managing. Training of all types is popular along with performance management and working parties.

■ *Evangelical Management:* This is management by mission statement, the latter being a set of vague but PC commitments to all sorts of moral, ethical and environmental issues currently in vogue. "It should be clear to visitors who read this document that they have entered a corporate heaven in which those fortunate enough to gain admission will spend blissful hours, enviably occupied in bringing good things to more people" (McKibbin, 1998: 21).

■ *Homoeopathic Management:* As most people know, homoeopathic remedies are universal because they produce symptoms like those of the disorder they are intended to cure. Thus one calls in bureaucratically minded people to deal with problems of excessive form filling and time wasting; thus one hires others to help with problems of over-staffing.

■ *Hostage Management:* A hostage is someone willing to sacrifice his or her career for yours. This style involves managers putting other people in trouble spots rather than dealing with it themselves. If these "plants" surprisingly succeed, the hostage manager can take the credit for strategic decision-making; if they fail, it must be put down to operational misjudgement by the hostage.

- *Inflation Management:* This is the making-a-mountain-out-of-a-molehill approach. Everything is inflated – success and failure. Grand certificates are given after training courses. The training center becomes the company university. The 100-volume library is an information center and, most important of all, job titles enjoy massive and meaningless inflation.

- *Lifeboat Management:* This occurs when the organization is in crisis and appoints various committees to analyze the problem. Once the call for equal sacrificing occurs it is done so enthusiastically that too much and too many are thrown overboard. The remaining people are so obsessed by jettisoning for the future that they completely lose the sense of what they should be doing.

- *Meddle Management:* A "hands on" approach that involves "compulsively and perpetually altering, fidgeting and tampering, a monstrous regiment of tinkers, meddlers and fiddlers whose ill-timed and misguided interference is ruining many a business" (McKibbin, 1998: 35). Gurus may be good meddle managers, advocating changes, relocations and restructuring again and again.

- *Narcissus Management:* Management that is obsessively concerned with its own image. Focus is on PR image – portraying one and finding out what others think. Forget the real business, the product, the customers' needs. Managers are concerned more with their popularity than with their effectiveness.

- *News Management:* This is management communication by news broadcast. Nothing is too trivial, irrelevant or obscure to be made newsworthy. There is an obsessive concern with blowing up all issues to make them important.

- *Obstruction Management:* The managers rejoice in preventing others from doing anything. They always mention safety (health and safety at work) or discrimination or new European legislation, or other powerful words that allow them to obstruct any good idea or policy that may benefit the company as a whole.

- *Placebo Management:* This is management via the "boardroom lunch"; the "staff committee" where people are made to feel better although nothing actually happens. These activities make both sides feel better because they believe that real communication occurs, although neither side talks honestly and nothing ever results.

- *Prosthetic Management:* This is the replacement of intelligence by prosthetic electronic gadgets. Thus certain computers can help people who cannot spell or draw: "All that now remains is for science to devise a prosthetic replacement for the ability to read, a machine that is able to scan and speak a printer text, eliminating at a stroke the unfair advantages currently suffered by those who cannot read" (McKibbin, 1998: 58).

- *Puppet Management:* This is management through others, not unlike ventriloquists' dummies. They write speeches, feed ideas and ultimately pull the strings of others. This may suit both parties – puppet and puppeteer – until the former is required to mouth something that is deeply controversial.

- *Signal Management:* Signal managers are more concerned with appearances than reality and are most concerned with sending the wrong kind of signal. They are concerned more with form than content; with interpretation rather than the consequence of the signal.

- *Territorial Management:* These managers are like fierce animals that adopt strange, aggressive tactics to warn and ward off trespassers: "Within an organization, savage inter-necine battles for territory are waged with memoranda, reports, position papers and incessant lobbying activities" (McKibbin, 1998: 25). The idea is to expand your department, take over another's territory.

- *Virtual Management:* This is management by elaborate charade that is little concerned with better products or services. It is a collusion between manager and employee where meetings are held, jobs defined and evaluations performed, but little or nothing is done.

- *Zoological Management:* This takes various forms:
    - *Hamster Management:* Industrious, obstinate, energetic but unable to learn from experience.
    - *Seagull Management:* Flying in from head office just long enough to crap over hard-working provincials and fly back to the nest.
    - *Locust Management:* A technique used to strip every asset of a company, leaving it picked clean of every morsel.
    - *Peacock Management:* A proud strutting manager that appears sleek and complacent but suddenly flies off to loftier perches.
    - *Rabbit Management:* The idea is to reproduce as much as possible: to copy parent company style all around the world; acquire subsidies and replicate oneself enthusiastically.

All of us recognize the incompetent manager in these different styles. Some organizations favor one over another. The joke, of course, is that each in their different ways is either bad, sad or mad. The tragedy is that not only are these manager styles common but that they are tacitly approved and perpetuated in various organizations. Whilst they would never of course use these labels they may well advocate the styles of management described. Worse still they model this behavior for others and even advocate it.

Missions

The first President Bush got a bit confused over the then current fad for mission statements. He called them "The Mission Thing". How was it different from the "vision thing" or the "objective thing"? Alas, this is not clear.

Companies exist to make money for their shareholders. Public companies exist to perform particular functions well. Hopefully they are efficient, effective and energetic as well as up to date, thorough and uncorrupt.

But most organizations are not content to quietly go about their important and difficult business. Inspired by a lethal combination of management gurus, narcissistic managers and PR specialists we have seen the emergence first of mission statements. Even quiet family firms and charities appear to have succumbed to this apparent need.

Mission statements are supposedly to explain what companies are trying to achieve. Presumably all public companies have as their bottom line to increase the value of shareholders' shares. They hope to be responsible, law-abiding and successful.

But over the years, vague moral statements have appeared in mission statements. Mission statements have become longer, woollier and what is often unrecognized, mutually contradictory. That is, they say they are often after possibly incompatible aims.

What might increase employee happiness may reduce shareholder value. How could one "delight" suppliers without increasing costs? Trade-offs have to be made in the short and the long term. Anderson (2000) has written a critical and important critique of mission statements entitled "*Good Companies Don't Have Missions*". His argument is that the first change is that shareholders have become stakeholders. Stakeholders apparently include shareholders, employees, customers, the local community, and so on. Of course, what employees feel able to deliver and what customers want may be complete opposites. Equally the local community may vigorously oppose expansion which is the primary aim of the shareholders. In fact in many mission statements obligation to the shareholder seems forgotten. Conflicting interests are never considered. The problem with serving the whole community is the same as serving all customers: it is impossible because they frequently have very different beliefs, preferences and demands. In short, different stakeholders have different objectives. They may be completely contradictory.

Some mission statements imply the business of the company is to save the world and/or to act as a sort of employee enrichment scheme. They imply everyone is in happy partnership (suppliers, customers, employees) to achieve this end. Further in the long list of missions it is not clear which is more (or less) important, when and why.

More and more mission statements use quasi-ethical and moral concepts like integrity, responsibility or morality. Some echo slightly out-of-date management jargon terms like: empowerment, potential, best practice.

Grandiloquent vacuity? Harmless fun? Foolish? Over-promising? What is wrong with drafting a mission statement? Many things according to Anderson (2000).

First, *they take time*. Some organizations organize workshops, away-days and focus groups at all levels to debate, absorb and, worse, "live" the mission statement. After the painful and expensive series of meetings both of the company mission statement there remains the urge on the part of some for each department to have their own specialized vision-mission thing. Mission statement consultants stalked the corridors of companies eager to stimulate the market in mission statements. More time, more motherhood and apple-pie: fewer tangible results.

Next, mission statements *don't fool people*. Long, politically correct, mission statements fool few. They do not make up for poor management, poor returns or dubious business aims.

Thirdly, they fundamentally *misrepresent the whole point of the organization*. Companies are not there as charitable, welfare institutions trying to spread health and happiness. They may do so, but they are there primarily to increase their value for the shareholders. Promise something different that one cannot, or worse (really) intends not to deliver, and it may easily cause a consumer backlash.

Too many claims for ethical behavior and values too often and one *invites challenge*. They are different contradictory ethical systems. The allocation of scarce resources may involve moral and economics issues. But it is naive to assume that there is a clear distinction between ethical (investing) and non-ethical behavior.

Most companies adhere to the basic principles of democratic capital-ism. They are enterprises in the political and economic sense and survive in the long run.

Evasive, vacuous, over-promising language can encourage a backlash by both employees and customers. This is often the case around issues like open-ness, transparency, accountability and integrity. At times of change, restruc-turing or acquisition managers are often devious and "political" to help the process. Paradoxically, they trumpet the idea that the change will lead to more transparency but are hypocritically the opposite in trying to achieve that end.

Just as there is the letter of the law and the spirit of the law so there is the hoped for behavior of the mission statement and the real behavior of the managers. Staff soon realize how things work – what is rewarded and what is punished. The rhetoric of the mission statements, the output of the PR department and the period talk about visions are, for the most part, qui-etly ignored. And so they should be.

References

Anderson, D. (2000). *Good Companies Don't Have Missions.* London: SAU.

McKibbin, S. (1998). *A Cynic's Guide to Management.* London: Robert Hale.